ADVENTURE TIME™

FINN & JAKE'S

Official Guide

PUFFIN

PUFFIN BOOKS

Published by the Penguin Group: London, New York, Australia,
Canada, India, Ireland, New Zealand and South Africa

Penguin Books Ltd, Registered Offices:
80 Strand, London WC2R ORL, England

puffinbooks.com

First published 2014
001

Written by Jake Black

Made and printed in China

ISBN: 978-0-141-35237-4

WELCOME TO

Ooo

WELCOME TO THE LAND OF OOO! It's pretty much the most mathematical place ever. It's filled with crazy people and a ton of kingdoms and we have super-awesome, kick-butt adventures all the time! I mean, c'mon, where else can you rescue a princess, get magical powers, and go to a mysterious underworld all in, like, a day?

We made this radical book so you can learn all about Ooo, too. We'll show you all the great places and people, and even give heroic advice so you can live like Finn and me!

OH MY GLOB! There's, like, a snail hidden on every double page, too. Can you find them all?

CONTENTS

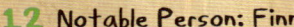

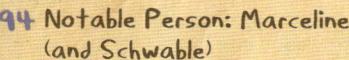

92 MOUNTAIN KINGDOM

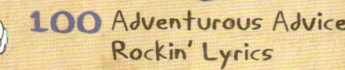

106 LUMPY SPACE

126 FIRE KINGDOM

OTHER PLACES

A BRIEF HISTORY OF

Ooo

So, you're probably wondering how we got here, in the Land of Ooo. We'll tell you. Um . . . actually, we can't. All we do know is that a thousand years ago, there was a huge war. MEGA WAR. Epic. It was called the Great Mushroom War and nobody really knows anything about it. Our friend Marceline and the Ice King remember seeing some huge cloud that looked like a mushroom. It killed everything, which was kinda dirtballs.

But then the people in Ooo happened. We don't know how they happened, either. But all of a sudden there were candy people and lumpy people and all the other kinds of people.

So they DEFINITELY happened, dude.

6

They divided the Land of Ooo into the kingdoms and areas it is today. They made the Candy Kingdom because everything was made of candy. They had the Ice Kingdom because everything was frozen. The Fire Kingdom because everything was volcanoes and fire and lava. And . . . you get the idea. People have just kinda lived where they feel the most comfortable. If you're a candy person, you probably want to live in the Candy Kingdom. Made of the Flame? The Fire Kingdom. Duh.

We've heard this place was called 'Earth' before the Mushroom War. We don't know where Ooo would have been located on Earth exactly, but we know that the rest of the world just exploded. Now the kingdoms are all ruled by different royal families and rulers.

My FAVOURITE ruler is PRINCESS BUBBLEGUM from the Candy Kingdom, but we'll talk about her later.

Basically, Ooo happened because of the Mushroom War. Some people think the Mushroom War was lame. But if it didn't happen, we wouldn't have the Land of Ooo, and you already know how we feel about that!

Check out this sweet map of the Land of Ooo. It'll help you figure out where everything is. For example, the Grass Lands are where we live. And the Fire Kingdom is the worst place ever. There are tons of other places in the land, too. Some that we've probably not even seen yet. (Well, maybe Finn hasn't seen them. I'm pretty sure I've seen it all.)

GRASS LANDS

Our first stop on our tour of the Land of Ooo is the Grass Lands, because it's where we live. It's the best part. It's got radical green grass and blue skies and the weather is always nice.

> Except when there are **KNIFE STORMS**.

It's not a thousand degrees like the Fire Kingdom or butt-freezing cold like the Ice Kingdom. It's just right. The Fire Kingdom and the Ice Kingdom are right next to the Grass Lands, though, so we never have to go very far to find an adventure. A lot of the time, adventure finds us. At home. When we want to be relaxing. Stupid adventure.

The weirdest thing about the Grass Lands is that there are two other little kingdoms inside it. The Hot Dog People Kingdom and the Goblin Kingdom. Totally weird that they'd be here in the middle of another place.

Remember that one time when you were king of the goblins, Finn? Sounds pretty cool, but actually turned out to be not much fun. Those goblins were weird.

SO WEIRD.

The point is, the Grass Lands is home and it's totally math. Our Tree House is amazing. The grass is beautiful. Our friends live nearby. And we can go on adventures whenever we freakin' want. Nothing we like more than kicking Ice King's butt.

TRUST POUND!

MORE INFO

RULER: Jake and Finn! (Unofficially.)

INHABITANTS: Jake, Finn, BMO, The Hot Dog People, Goblins, Tree Trunks.

GEOGRAPHY: Grassy, looks good, borders Candy Kingdom, Ice Kingdom and Fire Kingdom.

CLIMATE: Warm, sunny, with rainbows. Occasional knife storms.

NOTABLE PERSON

FINN

RAD FACTOR 10

It's Adventure Time!

Mathematical!

I want BIONIC LEGS.

NAME: Finn.

SPECIES: Human.

HOME: The Tree Fort in the Grass Lands.

DON'T tell Finn I said this, cos he'd probably be weirded out, but I love that guy. **HE'S MY BEST PAL AND ALWAYS WILL BE.**

Biography: (Written by Jake)

So, my parents found Finn in the woods when he was just a baby and raised him as their own. As the only human in all of the Land of Ooo, Finn is the greatest warrior in the history of everything. He fights hard to win every battle he's in and he's got mad skills as an adventurer. He loves using his many swords and crossbows to battle villains.

Everyone knows he has a mad crush on Princess Bubblegum and maybe someday he'll be her boyfriend.

Sure. If you say so, dude.

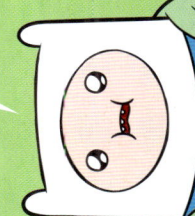

He's got a lot of enemies, but that's good because it shows that he's the most epically righteous guy ever. He's still got some growing up to do, but I'm always there to help him learn about the world.

Can you tell I didn'- write that part?

MORE INFO

CATEGORY: Best friend.

APPEARANCE: Human with blonde hair. He's missing some teeth from biting rocks and stuff.

ACCESSORIES: His famous white hat, his swords and crossbows.

PERSONALITY: Brave, righteous warrior. Definitely not wrongteous.

POWERS: No special powers, except awesome amounts of bravery and courage.

LIKES AND DISLIKES: Likes Princess Bubblegum, going on adventures and defeating bad guys. Dislikes the Ice King and anyone not as righteous as he is.

DO SAY: "Let's go on an adventure!"

DON'T SAY: "I'm better than you at _____."

* Rad factor is a scale we made up. Really rad is 10. Totally not rad is 1. We're a 10. <u>Go figure.</u>

NOTABLE PERSON

JAKE

My subconscious must be hungry, HUH?

SLEDS ARE FOR SUCKERS! Just ride on my gut!

EASY PEASY, livin' greasy!

NAME: Jake.

SPECIES: Magical Dog.

HOME: The Tree Fort in the Grass Lands.

Biography: (Written by Finn)

Jake is the best sidekick anyone could ever have. He hates when I call him a sidekick, but what's he gonna do? He is a sidekick!

We're kind of brothers since his parents saved and raised baby me. When we fight bad guys together, his powers are super helpful. He can stretch like a million miles long, and twist his body, blow it up big, morph into stuff. It's soooo sweet. When we get our butts kicked, Jake knows how to make me feel better with a joke or something like that. He's really laid back and he thinks he'll live like another hundred years. That's pretty sweet if you think about it. Dogs live a long time when they're magic.

I'm glad Jake's my brother. AND especially my SIDEKICK.

I'm not your SIDEKICK.

MORE INFO

CATEGORY: Best friend.

APPEARANCE: A yellow/orange dog with giant eyes.

ACCESSORIES: He wears invisible pants. That's why you can't see them — they're invisible. But he's totally wearing them!

PERSONALITY: Relaxed, an easy-going guy, but protective of his family and friends.

POWERS: Can stretch his body into almost any shape. Can shrink until he's almost invisible too. When he does this awesome move, his organs move into his thumb.

LIKES AND DISLIKES: Likes playing video games, adventuring, writing a newspaper column called 'Begs the Question.' He also likes to eat. A lot. Including crazy stuff like the Everything Burrito.

DO SAY: "Food time!"

DON'T SAY: "You're my favourite sidekick!"

BMO

> I am incapable of emotion, but you are making me ticked!

> Who wants to play video games?

> I feel like I got hit with a Dracula by King Kong.

NAME: BMO (Pronounced 'Beemo'), likes us to call him 'Sensei'.

SPECIES: Living Computer/Video Game System.

HOME: Tree Fort in the Grass Lands.

Biography:

BMO is awesome. He's pretty much everything we ever need. He's a video game console, a camera, a video-editing system, a flashlight and a movie player. Pretty much anything electronic. Sometimes he's also a she. It depends on what game we're playing, or what mood BMO's in.

> Either way, BMO makes for great company.

BMO's also got some weird stuff going on in his brain, or circuit board, or whatever's inside. Like, when he talks to himself in the mirror, he calls mirror-BMO 'Football.' What? Messed up, we know. What's even more messed up is when BMO tries to teach 'Football' manners and junk. Like the reflection needs to learn manners. Oh well. BMO's still cool. And super-helpful around the house. He's great at cooking, cleaning and lots of other stuff.

> But his best part is being
> **VIDEO GAMES.**

MORE INFO

CATEGORY: Friend.

APPEARANCE: BMO pretty much looks like your favourite video game system. Has a large video screen for a face and a bunch of control buttons and slots on his green outer shell.

ACCESSORIES: Two game-controlling joysticks.

PERSONALITY: Very loyal and protective of his awesome roommates. Happy and really smart.

POWERS: Can play video games and perform loads of cool computing and electronic-type tasks.

LIKES AND DISLIKES: Likes hot chocolate. Dislikes it when people remove his outer shell or crack his screen.

DO SAY: "Let's play some video games!"

DON'T SAY: "Time to clean your screen."

TREE TRUNKS

C'mon boys! I made y'all some APPLE PIE!

Where's my dang APPLES?

The tea party was CRUMMIER than a big ol' BISCUIT!

She's a good friend and a great cook, but she went INSANE that one time.

NAME: Tree Trunks.

SPECIES: Elephant (Quartzion the Crystal Queen — temporarily, in the Crystal Dimension).

HOME: Candy Kingdom.

RAD FACTOR 7 RAD FACTOR

Biography:

Tree Trunks. Oh boy. This is awkward. Tree Trunks is our friend and all, but one time she went crazy and became the queen of the Crystal Dimension. That made her look at Finn in a TOTALLY different way. I mean, she loves cooking. We totally support that. She especially likes making apple pies, and we love eating apple pies. But when she bit into the Crystal Gem Apple and it sent her to the Crystal Dimension, where she went nuts and wanted Finn to rule with her? Not cool. Good thing we rescued her from the depths of insanity, so he didn't have to be the king!

> Yeah. She's super-duper nice, though.

> Yeah, she's nice. And she's in love with Mr. Pig, which is cool.

MORE INFO

CATEGORY: Friend.

APPEARANCE: A small, round, yellow elephant.

ACCESSORIES: Tree Trunks wears a lot of make-up.

PERSONALITY: Known for being super-nice and friendly to all, Tree Trunks is kind to pretty much everyone, except when she goes insane in the Crystal Dimension.

POWERS: Can stretch her trunk and use it to spray water at enemies. Also makes amazing apple pies.

LIKES AND DISLIKES: Likes cooking, especially baking. Really likes Mr. Pig. Dislikes going crazy in the Crystal Dimension.

DO SAY: "This apple pie is amazing!"

DON'T SAY: "Whoa! Too much make-up!"

TREE FORT

Everybody needs a sweet place to live and keep their junk. Ours is the Tree Fort. It sounds like it's small when we call it that — Tree Fort. It's actually GIGANTIC. Like SUPER GIGANTIC. It's an entire tree. Somebody turned the tree into a house like a zillion years ago. Our friend Marceline lived in it once, way before we did. You're totes jealous of its awesomeness, aren't you?

Let's take you on a tour of our house. The base of the tree, the trunk, (not to be confused with our friend Tree Trunks who's an elephant) is where we keep all our loot from adventures. Seriously, there's sweet stuff in there. But **DON'T STEAL FROM US. IF YOU DO, WE'LL HUNT YOU DOWN AND FIND YOU . . .**

We're just kidding. But DON'T STEAL OUR TREASURE from the tree trunk.

Our favourite part of the Tree Fort is our bedroom. That's where we sleep. Finn's bed is amazing. It's so comfortable. There's not much he likes more than crawling into bed after a day full of tough adventures. As long as there's no worms. He hates it when worms get in his bed. Wouldn't you? It's so gross. It gets him mad. Way mad. No worms in the bed!

Jake's bed is pretty cool, too. It's a drawer. But that's just how he likes it. It lets him be close to his favourite possessions. You know, stuff like his viola. Plus, it's comfortable, too. He doesn't need to stretch out after an adventure. Usually he stretches out during the adventure and by the time he's ready to sleep, the last thing he wants to do is any more stretching!

You know what I also love in our house? The kitchen. I like to eat and the kitchen has all our rad food. Awesome place to hang out! And eat.

The living room is where we play RAD video games with BMO. We do other stuff in there too. Like watch movies. Or be bored. It's got couches and stuff where we can sit.

I think they know what couches are for, Finn.

OK. I'll be quiet.

The Tree Fort has everything else that an awesome house needs. A bathroom, a yard, a ladder nailed to the outside so we can climb up to our bedroom. Probably all just like your house. Except our house has a weapons room full of weapons. What did you think was in there? Lollipops? The lollipops are all in the Candy Kingdom. Our Tree Fort is really close to the border of the Candy Kingdom, which is crazy convenient for going on adventures there and rescuing Princess Bubblegum and stuff.

Princess Bubblegum...

So basically the Tree Fort is MATHEMATICAL. Probably the most rhombus place in Ooo. We wouldn't want to live anywhere else. Not a castle, or some weird place like Tree Trunks' house, with pink stripes and stuff.

Especially not a castle. Finn was a king once and it was wrongteous. This place is the best. And we'll fight anyone who disagrees or wants to take it away from us! **TREE FORT ALL THE WAY!**

TREE FORT!
TREE FORT!
TREE FORT!

FRIENDSHIP

A lot of people ask us how come we have such **AWESOME ADVENTURES** and I always tell them that it's because Finn and I understand the first rule of adventuring. Always have a buddy with you, and don't lose your buddy along the way. Finn is always my buddy, and I'm always his . . .

SIDEKICK. You're always my SIDEKICK.

DUDE, WHAT? I taught you everything you know, but not everything I know. If anyone's a sidekick, it's **YOU**, pal. I mean, if it weren't for me, **YOU WOULDN'T HAVE SURVIVED** being a baby in the forest.

OK. We're best friends not sidekicks. And best friends stick together through thick and thin. Through adventures and battles. WE'RE ALWAYS THERE FOR EACH OTHER. NEVER LEAVE YOUR FRIEND BEHIND.

One of our best friends is **BMO**. BMO's a good friend to us because he's always got our backs. If anything bad happens to us, BMO's gonna help us out. That's what we call a friend. Plus, BMO's fun and we have a lot in common with her . . . him . . . BMO. We like to play video games – BMO <u>is</u> video games.

Hanging out in our living room playing video games with BMO and my sidekick is the BEST.

I. AM. NOT. A. SIDEKICK.

If you have more than one best friend, don't try to make all your best friends be friends with each other. They might not get along. Like if Marceline and Princess Bubblegum and Lumpy Space Princess wanted to hang out, and we were like, sure, but then they had a fight . . . that would be awkward for us.

Having a lot of friends can be good. We're pretty much friends with everybody. Except for, like, Ice King. I hate that guy. If you want to know who our friends are, you can check out the list at the back of this book. That's almost everybody!

FRIENDSHIP

It's important to be able to share stuff with your friends – especially your best friends! You gotta tell them what's going on with you and make sure you know what's going on with them. When you're good friends with someone, you end up knowing loads of stuff about them – maybe even secret stuff no one else knows!

Huh? Like what, man?

Like how you're afraid of the ocean.

HEY, SHUT UP! That's a real phobia – thalassophobia, look it up! Anyway, your insides are cursed to smell like vanilla. And you get totally freaked out by spiders.

Dude, so do you! AND when you were a baby, you made up this crazy waggling butt-dance to a song that went, 'I'm a buff baby, that can dance like a man! I can shake-ah my booty . . .'

BRO, ENOUGH!

OK, so, it doesn't have to be embarrassing stuff that you know about each other – it can be cool stuff, too. Like, I know that Finn is freakishly good at origami. And he's a sweet beat-boxer. AND one time, he swallowed a tiny computer, so he can autotune his own voice. When he does, it sounds seriously awesome.

Hey, thanks dude! I guess there's a load of algebraic stuff I know about you, too. Like how you're the MOST RADICAL skateboarder ever. And you have an impressive eye-patch collection. And you're a kick-butt writer – you even write that nerdy newspaper column, 'Begs the Question'!

See. We know ALL the stuff about each other. Like best bros should.

ADVICE

BEGS THE QUESTION
by JAKE

Rhombus!

REMEMBER THE TIME?

Lots of fun stuff has happened around the Grass Lands. Like, remember that time we wanted to go out of the house and have an adventure, but there was a knife storm and we ended up doing stuff in the house? And then you said we should use our imaginations, which I thought was lame, but then your imagination became real. And the floor turned to lava and a troll tried to destroy us. You finally got it under control, though, and everything returned to normal. It kinda made me not want to hang out alone in the house any more.

Yeah, that was a good time. Do you remember that time when you were all bummed out because Princess Bubblegum thought you were acting weird, and you got all depressed and stuff? So I went out to find you a girlfriend and brought Flame Princess to the house? Well, I guess she followed me back and torched the place because she was mad at me. She got you to notice her, though. So I guess that worked out kinda good. It helped you forget about Princess Bubblegum for a minute.

DUDE, IT WAS A DISASTER! One thing I really would like to forget is how your dad, Joshua, built a dungeon to toughen me up. Seriously, who does that? Builds a dungeon for their baby kids to be in? I mean, your dad was super-cool and I love him and everything, but c'mon, a dungeon?

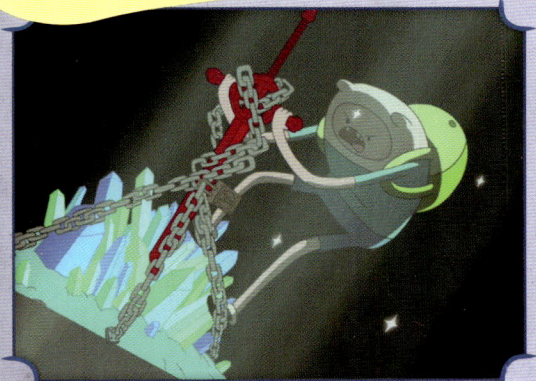

Yeah, but it worked, right? You're tough and the greatest warrior in the entire Land of Ooo, so it's no bigs! You should be HAPPY my dad did the whole dungeon thing. YOU BIG BABY.

BONUS ENCOUNTERS

When you travel around the Grass Lands, there are some people that you might meet or you might not. It's hard to say. They're like rare or something. If you do see them, though, put a tick mark in the box next to their picture.

THE SNAIL ☐

You never know where the snail will show up. It might be on your head, or maybe in a tree, or possibly in an epic battle. But he's always around somewhere. If you can spot him on your journeys through the Land of Ooo, you'll be one of only a special few to actually notice him. Be careful, though, because he gets possessed by evil sometimes!

HOT DOG PEOPLE ☐

The Hot Dog People are actually kind of easy to find in the Grass Lands, because they all live in the Hot Dog Kingdom, which is tiny - it's a little bit of grass and a doghouse. They look like a mix of hot dogs (the food) and dogs (the animals). Do you think that's weird? Don't let them know that. The Hot Dog People think they're all important and noble, but they're actually kinda dumb and get scared real easy.

BANANA MAN □

This is the elusive and sort-of-mysterious Banana Man. The odds are you won't run into him in the Grass Lands, but you might. I think we'll cross paths with the Banana Man again someday, so who's to say you won't, too? He likes to build spaceships, and one time he helped me, Finn and BMO fix a truck. Smart.

SHELBY □

Shelby is a worm-like creature who lives inside Jake's viola. So that means that Shelby is a crazy-hard resident of the Grass Lands to see, unless you can catch a peek at Jake's viola. Shelby is friends with me, Jake, and everyone else in the Candy Kingdom, it seems like! So if you do meet up, I'm pretty sure you'll be friends, too.

- BMO's -
Game Guide

Hello! BMO here. I'm sooooo excited that Finn and Jake invited me to talk a little bit about the Land of Ooo in their book, especially video games. I love those guys and I love video games, mostly because I am video games. Here are some of the best games people can play with me.

Adventure Master

This one's super-difficult. Finn and Jake try really hard to beat this game. They sometimes get a little bit frustrated. I can't help them because of the video game code. But when they win and become Adventure Masters, that's the best!

Pro Football 1861

Ever wonder what it would be like if Abraham Lincoln battled Abraham Lincoln in a sports video game? I like this game because it has a rainbow in it. And Abraham Lincoln. Whoever that is. I've heard he's cool.

–099   CPU–099

Bug Battle

This one isn't quite as hard for Jake and Finn, but some people get really mad when they lose. You win by killing a lot of spiders and giant bugs. You know, kind of like when Finn and Jake go on adventures in real life.

Kompy's Kastle

This is Jake's favouritest game. He's one of the best players at it ever. He has one of the highest scores in all of the Land of Ooo. This game has a lot of battles, and is all about Kompy. Sometimes you can even play two players and fight each other! I don't like it when Finn and Jake fight each other. I like it when they fight together against bad guys in my video games or even in the real world. But nobody better hurt then because I love those guys and if anybody does hurt then, I'll get then!

KOMPY'S KASTLE
1 PLAYER
2 PLAYER CO-OP

KRUSH IT KOMPY

Oh dear! I think I got a little distracted thinking about my friends! Where was I?

BMO's Game Guide

That's right, I was telling you about the games that can be played with me.

Guardians of Sunshine

In this game you fight a lot of monsters. Scary monsters who are really hard to beat in the game. Finn and Jake tried with all their might playing out in the real world, but they wanted to beat the bad guys so bad that they convinced me to have them fight inside the game itself. It made them digital, but they got what they wanted. They were able to defeat the monsters in the game forever!

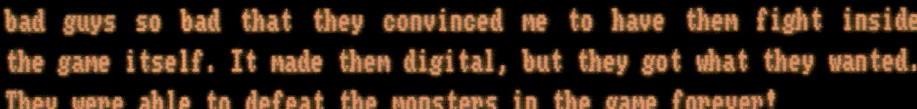

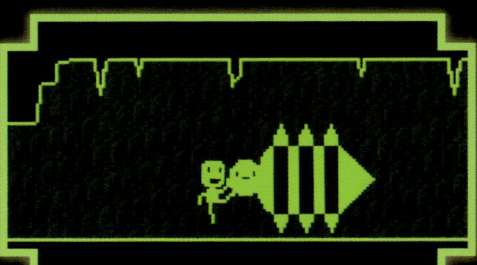

Conversation Parade

This game lets me talk to the players. I like it when Finn and Jake play this game because then I get to talk to them. They pretty much hate the game, though, so we don't ever really play it.

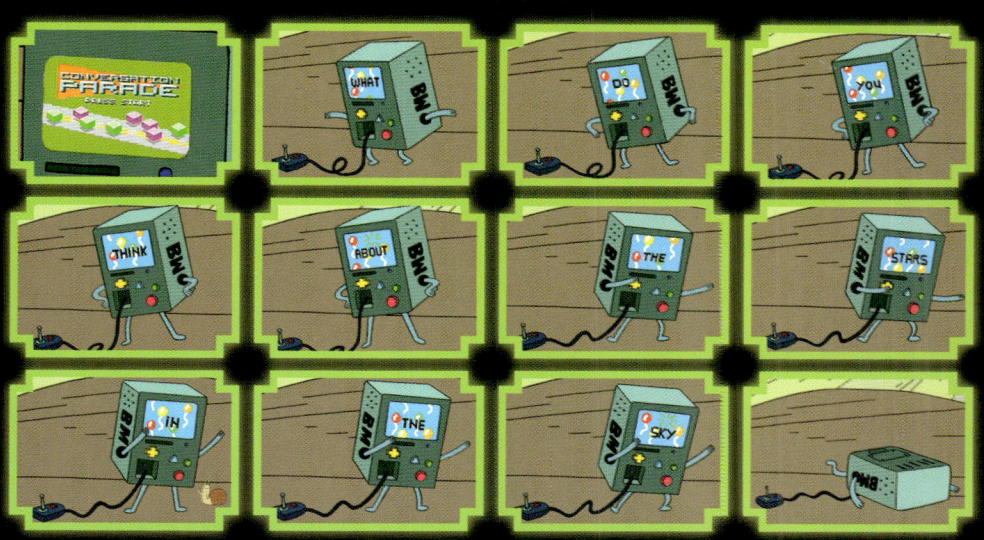

There's lots of other games you can play, but I don't want to list all of them. That's too much. Especially when I can tell you about the other things I can do. I can make movies, play movies, make toast, shine light in the dark, and lots of other stuff! I have a lot of circuits and I need batteries. I tell people that I don't have emotions, but sometimes I can't help displaying a smile.

Jake and Finn are the most important people in the world to me. I'll let other people play my games, but I like it best when Jake and Finn play because they're my best friends. And best friends should play video games with each other.

Oh! By the way, I like to play games, too. Not video games. Just real life games. Where I pretend stuff. Like where I'm a real boy. Or a tough detective. They're fun. But mostly I play those games when I'm alone. They're better that way.

CANDY KINGDOM

RULER: Princess Bubblegum.

INHABITANTS: The Candy People, Princess Bubblegum, Earl of Lemongrab, Peppermint Butler, Lady Rainicorn.

GEOGRAPHY: Everything is made of sugar and totally pink. Cotton Candy Forest is part of the kingdom. Actually the Grass Lands are owned by the Candy Kingdom, too.

CLIMATE: Warm, righteous, sweet (literally), happy all the time.

Lots of our adventures take place in the Candy Kingdom because we live close to it, but also because it's awesome. Everything is made of candy. How can you beat that? The Grass Lands are technically part of the Candy Kingdom, so we pretty much live in it, even though the Grass Lands and Tree Fort aren't made of candy. We pay taxes to the Candy Kingdom, but we don't know what we pay them for. It's not like the police or the military are any good.

We have to fight all their battles for them!

Well, the main reason we have to fight their battles for them is because the Candy Kingdom is on the border of pretty much every other kingdom, and when those other kingdoms' evil rulers want something to do, they attack the Candy Kingdom. Then it's up to us to protect Princess Bubblegum and the rest of the kingdom from all evil.

Yeah, my favourite thing is protecting the kingdom from lousy wormy sneaky sneaks like the Ice King.

We like being in the Candy Kingdom because there's way fun stuff to do there, too. Like going to science barbecues. And hanging out with Princess Bubblegum.

Jake also has a lady friend who lives in the Candy Kingdom, Lady Rainicorn. They have some kids together, but they grew up fast, so he doesn't see them very much. But he likes living close by so he can see them sometimes. And her.

PRINCESS BUBBLEGUM

That's it! The answer was so simple, I was too smart to see it!

She's one of our favourite people, but she's not Jake or Finn so she's not a perfect 10.

RAD FACTOR 9 RAD FACTOR

You can't break royal promises! Never, ever, never, no matter what, forever!

Listen, all magic is scientific principals presented like 'mystical hoodoo' which is fun, but it's sort of irresponsible.

NAME: Princess Bubblegum, first name Bonnibel (nicknames include PB, P-Bubs, Peebles).

SPECIES: Candy Person.

HOME: Candy Kingdom.

Biography:

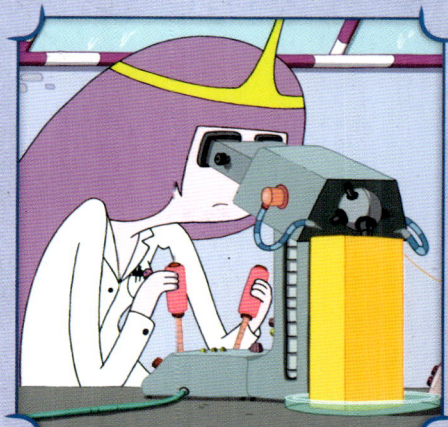

Princess Bubblegum is one pretty cool Candy gal. She's super-smart and an awesome friend. She loves the people of the Candy Kingdom and is an excellent ruler because she's not too mean. She's good. Plus Finn is in love with her, even though he tried dating Flame Princess for a while.

> I'm... uh... not totally in love with her. Just kind of.

He still digs Flame Princess, they just weren't meant to be. Princess Bubblegum is pretty close to perfect and he just likes being around her, even if she's way smarter than him. And she never really like, 'like' liked him back. She did cut his face with scissors once, which kind of screwed things up between them.

> But I still think she's awesome, in a non-hooking-up kinda way.

MORE INFO

CATEGORY: Friend.

APPEARANCE: Pink, bubblegummy princess.

ACCESSORIES: Crown, sometimes a cool lab coat and goggles.

PERSONALITY: Happy, supportive, friendly — unless you mess with her, then she gets really, really angry.

POWERS: Speaks many languages, very smart with science, lots of musical talent.

LIKES AND DISLIKES: Likes all ceremonies (especially tea ceremonies), being with her friends and science. Dislikes enemies and being lied to.

DO SAY: "Let's have a special ceremony for this."

DON'T SAY: "Girls aren't good at science."

LADY RAINICORN

NAME: Lady Rainicorn.

SPECIES: Rainicorn.

HOME: Candy Kingdom, a stable near the Candy Castle.

RAD FACTOR
10
RAD FACTOR

Korean: 와, 이 방은 예쁜 새 소리에 대한 내 사랑보다 더 크네!
English translation: 'Wow. This chamber is bigger than my love for the songs of pretty birds!'

Korean: 내 등에 올라 타! 나는 당신에게 집까지 태워 모두를 줄 것이다.
English translation: 'Hop on my back! I'll give you both a ride home.'

I know we said only me and Finn could be a 10. But I like her A LOT.

Biography:

Jake met Lady Rainicorn a while ago and they became friends because they both play the viola. He thinks she's the most beautiful, radical, wonderful, shmow-zow person in the whole Land of Ooo. The best part is, he also speaks Korean, like she does, so she doesn't need a universal translator all the time.

I met her parents one time. That made me really nervous. I dressed up as a rainicorn to try to impress them.

Jake totally loves her and together they have some rainicorn puppies. Their names are: TV, Charlie, Viola, Kim Kil Whan, and Jake, Jr. Those pups are magical. No, literally. They have magical powers that made them grow up fast. But Jake loves them like he loves their mother. Jake and Lady Rainicorn don't live together, because she has to live by the Candy Castle so she can be close to Princess Bubblegum.

I don't mind too much, though. I like living with my best bro, Finn.

MORE INFO

TRUST POUND!

CATEGORY: Jake's girlfriend.

APPEARANCE: A unicorn with a rainbow-creating body and long blonde hair. And big, round eyes.

ACCESSORIES: Horn, universal translator.

PERSONALITY: Very laid-back and easy-going. She is super-loyal, especially to Jake and Princess Bubblegum.

POWERS: Can blast energy from her horn, can fly, phases through walls, changes colours of stuff, speaks Korean (one of very few people in the Land of Ooo who can).

LIKES AND DISLIKES: Likes spending time with her children, Jake and Princess Bubblegum. Dislikes using a universal translator.

DO SAY: "You're a great mother."

DON'T SAY: "You're not strong enough to go on adventures or battle bad guys."

Biography:

Appearances can be deceptive. Peppermint Butler looks like someone who would be a good guy and he kinda is, but don't let that fool you. He's got a sugarload of evil in him. At least we think he does. No one knows for sure what his shady past is. All we know is that right now he's the butler for the Candy Castle, but in the past he had a weird connection to the dark magic worlds or something.

Apparently some people even call him 'the Dark One.' Wrongteous.

We think he controls his evil instincts pretty good and he can totally tell if someone is evil themselves, which is helpful for us on adventures. But we don't trust him. And neither should you. And don't make a deal with him about anything, because then he'll want your flesh.

Siiiick.

MORE INFO

CATEGORY: Servant of Princess Bubblegum.

APPEARANCE: He looks like a giant round peppermint candy with a suit on.

ACCESSORIES: A special bow tie that looks kinda snazzy with his little minty suit.

PERSONALITY: Boring! He's all like, 'These are the rules' and 'I'm here to serve you'.

POWERS: Can tap into the dark magic of the Land of the Dead. Can sense if a person is evil.

LIKES AND DISLIKES: Likes serving Princess Bubblegum. Dislikes people asking about his past.

DO SAY: "Can you tell us if he's evil?"

DON'T SAY: "You don't get to be the grillmeister."

EARL OF LEMONGRAB

This castle is in unacceptable condition! UNACCEPTABLE!

Twelve years dungeon. All of you. Dungeon. Seven years, no trials. C'mon, let's move it!

Awake! Avast! Hold tight your buns, if buns you do hold dear. For time has come to wake and run and not give way to fear!

NAME: Earl of Lemongrab.

SPECIES: Candy Person.

HOME: Castle Lemongrab.

Biography:

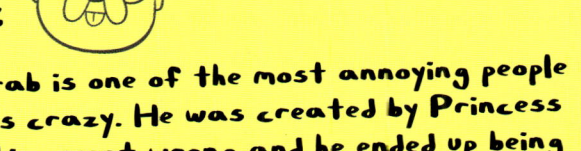

The Earl of Lemongrab is one of the most annoying people we've ever met. Dude's crazy. He was created by Princess Bubblegum but something went wrong and he ended up being totally nuts. He isn't nice to anyone. Ever.

Like, ever.

He wants to be the ruler of the Candy Kingdom. Princess Bubblegum made him the next in line for the throne, but he doesn't want to wait for her to die, so he keeps trying to overthrow her so he can rule.

That's dark, bro.

Princess Bubblegum made a second Earl of Lemongrab, Lemongrab 2, so the first one could have a friend. They lived together and had little lemon kids they made out of food. Lemongrab liked Lemongrab 2 because Lemongrab 2 understood Lemongrab. Still, he's totally obnoxious and we just kinda always want to kick his butt. Just to do it. Teach him some respect, and not to be so rude to everyone all the time.

HEY. YOU TWO. TEN YEARS DUNGEON!

What?! Lemongrab, get the glob out of our book!

UNACCEPTABLE!

MORE INFO

CATEGORY: Frenemy.

APPEARANCE: Humanoid, but with a lemon-shaped head. He has yellow skin with weird bumps, like a lemon.

ACCESSORIES: Carries a sword. Sometimes needs reading glasses.

PERSONALITY: Grouchy, sometimes mean and almost always socially clueless.

POWERS: Very strong and tough because of his rind-like skin, expert swordsman, very flexible.

LIKES AND DISLIKES: Likes pretty much nothing and dislikes pretty much everything.

DO SAY: "You have cute kids."

DON'T SAY: "You'll never be the ruler of the Candy Kingdom."

PRINCESS BUBBLEGUM'S CASTLE

In the middle of the Candy Kingdom is the Candy Castle, or as it's better known, Princess Bubblegum's Castle. It's your typical castle, since it's got a moat, a drawbridge, guards, an armoury and all that stuff.

What's different, though, is that it's made out of candy. You could eat it if you wanted, but you'd probably be arrested and thrown in the candy dungeon. Dungeons are the worst, even if they're made out of candy. Anyway, this is where Princess Bubblegum rules the Candy Kingdom from.

Sometimes the castle looks like it's melting because part of it is made out of delicious ice cream. Mmm. Ice cream. It's got a couple of giant statues at the front that are sorta standing guard. They blow bubbles, which is kinda cool.

The castle has a ton of rooms. We've only seen some of them. Like Princess Bubblegum's lab where she does all her experiments and junk. The door to the lab is made out of candy steel! There's also a massive kitchen where amazing food is made.

Mmm. Food.

The Great Hall is where Princess Bubblegum has her parties and ceremonies. If you look around the Candy Castle, you have to be careful where you go, because there's lots of secret passages and you can get lost or end up in the dungeon. Still, this place is sweet.

It's our favourite castle in the Land of Ooo. We adventure over there as often as we can to explore more of it.

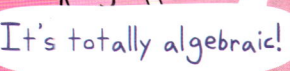

It's totally algebraic!

COTTON CANDY FOREST

One of the craziest places in the Candy Kingdom is the Cotton Candy Forest. It's a forest where the 'trees' are made out of cotton candy. Bet you never guessed that. Weird stuff happens in that forest. It's right next to the Desert of Doom and you can get to the Lumpy Space Kingdom by finding a frog and a mushroom in there. More about that later.

I know. It sounds crazy, but trust me. It works like that. Told you . . . weird stuff.

The Royal Tart Path goes over the forest, so if you ever walk that path, you'll see it. For some reason, people seem to really like the Cotton Candy Forest, but not Finn. Nothing really happens there except going to Lumpy Space. No adventures. And if it doesn't have adventures, he doesn't like going.

Jake likes the forest because Lady Rainicorn lives there in her royal stable with some of their pups. The Cotton Candy Forest will always be like his second home. Lady Rainicorn's stable is kinda small, but looks cool. It's in a clearing in the forest, so it's not surrounded by tons of cotton candy trees or anything. Jake uses Lady Rainicorn's powers to change the colours of stuff around the house. That's fun.

But it doesn't really matter to me what the house looks like. What matters to me is that the people I love most are there.

Lame.

ADVENTUROUS ADVICE

ROMANCE

So you already know that I hooked up with Lady Rainicorn. You gotta know how to be cool around the people you love, so I'm here to give you some pointers. Because I've been so successful at it, and pretty much all the other guys I know have failed. At least Finn and Ice King have.

> Whatever, dude. I'm good with the ladies.

> No, you're not. You had a major embarrassing crush on Princess Bubblegum and probably still do, but she's not interested in you. You dated Flame Princess, but that turned out even worse. So you need some advice and I'm the guy to give it to you.

First, you gotta be clean. No one likes anyone who is filthy all the time. I know you don't believe that but trust me, if you smell bad, it's over. So try to shower once in a while and maybe put on some cologne or something to make you smell like you didn't sleep in a monster's butt.

Next, remember that action and adventure are both cool. The absolute worst thing you can do is be boring or do boring stuff. Life is meant to be lived. It's meant to be explored. It's meant to be exciting. It's...

ADVENTURE TIME!

Yeah. It's Adventure Time. Adventures are good things to do if you go on a date, because if your date is tough like Lady Rainicorn, then she or he is totally worth being with. You don't wanna hang around with folks who can't do anything. Who get scared easy. You want them to be fun and exciting and tough and brave. You also want them to be smart.

All of those things are why I was in love with Princess Bubblegum.

You're still in love with her, dude.

REMEMBER THE TIME?

Sooooo many of our adventures have happened in the Candy Kingdom. I don't think I can even remember all of them, but I do remember some. Like remember the time Ricardio tried to get with Princess Bubblegum and we had to prove he was evil? Or the time that a black hole opened up and almost swallowed the whole kingdom? Or even the invasions of the Candy Kingdom by the Hyooman Tribe and the Penguins? We've even had a zombie apocalypse in the Candy Kingdom. Every time this stuff happens, though, Jake and I are there to save the day!

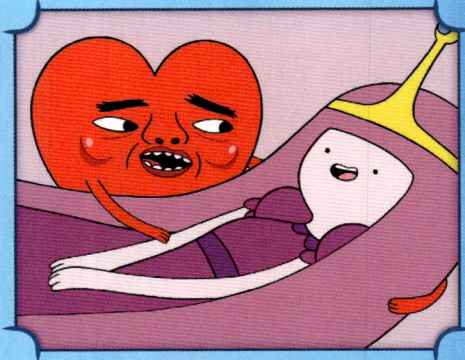

Remember the time when Earl of Lemongrab tried to overthrow the Princess and take over the Kingdom by making the Princess turn into a thirteen-year-old instead of an eighteen-year-old? That was an epic fail on his part because we saved the day that time, too! You're totally jealous you weren't there, aren't you?

Some of the best times we've had in the Candy Kingdom are when we've partied at the Candy Castle with the Princess and her friends. Like the science barbecue. That's one of my favourites, even though I kind of screwed it up by being too smart. Choose Goose gave me these super-nerdy magical glasses called the Glasses of Nerdicon, and then the extra-smart me accidentally created a weird dimensional shadow thing, which kinda caused time and space to collapse. It was my bad.

She forgave you in the end, though. In fact, your non-magical smartness saved everyone, so Princess Bubblegum thought you were some sort of hero. And she was happy that you'd made the barbecue exciting! I still don't get how you managed to come out of it the good guy. Weird.

BONUS ENCOUNTERS
CANDY PEOPLE

As with everything in the Candy Kingdom, the Candy People are made out of candy. There are many, many Candy People who live in the Candy Kingdom. As you explore it, you may run into some of these most prominent citizens. They are my friends and countrymen.

BANANA GUARD ☐

Members of the Candy Kingdom Police Force, the Banana Guards look how they sound — like bananas, who are also guards. Their flesh is not actually made of candy, but, as you can see, it's close enough.

GUMDROPS ☐

These sugary little folk make up most of the Candy Kingdom's population. The most famous of them are the Gumdrop Lasses, who wear neat little bows on their heads.

STARCHY ☐

A chocolate malt ball gravedigger, who does a lot of other odd jobs around the kingdom, including mail person and radio host. Farts when squeezed. Gross.

JELLY BEAN PEOPLE ☐

The Jelly Bean People are the royal cooks who make the royal tarts for Princess Bubblegum.

MR. CUPCAKE ☐

A super strong, athletic bloke, Mr. Cupcake is a chocolate cupcake who hangs out with Jake and Finn quite frequently.

DR. DEXTROSE, DR. ICE CREAM, AND DR. DONUT ☐

The medical staff of the Candy Kingdom. There have been times when these doctors have saved Princess Bubblegum, like when she was turned green by an evil potion, and the time when Dr. Ice Cream saved her by putting her in a milk suit.

NURSE POUNDCAKE ☐

Assists the doctors. Believes magic can heal Candy patients.

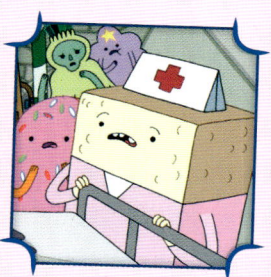

CANDY MAGICIAN ☐

A talented cookie-like magician who participates in the talent show held in the kingdom from time to time.

PRINCESS BUBBLEGUM'S GUIDE TO AWESOME CANDY HAPPENINGS

Finn and Jake asked me to tell you about some of the special events and ceremonies we have here in the Candy Kingdom. I am ever so happy to do this! I actually created the entire Candy Kingdom and all the events in it. I really enjoy events. They allow me to be with my Candy People friends and celebrate what a joy it is to live here in the Candy Kingdom.

Hey, PB, maybe you could write about the...

Shh, Finn! I'm talking now!

First up, let's talk about the Marshmallow Tea Ceremony. This is a special ceremony that only a very few people have successfully participated in. It involves drinking tea while bouncing on a huge tower of marshmallows. The tricky part is that you can't spill the tea while you bounce. Finn and Jake have tried it, but they aren't very good. Lumpy Space Princess and I are the best, because Lumpy Space Princess can float and I have spent a lifetime mastering it.

That dumb marshmallow ceremony is waaaay too hard.

BE QUIET, FINN! I'M EXPLAINING THINGS HERE!

Another of the Candy Kingdom Happenings I enjoy is the Back Rubbing Ceremony. This is one of the most special ceremonies that occurs in the Land of Ooo. It is only for the royals of the different kingdoms. We gather together in the Bad Lands and rub each other's backs. It feels very good and very relaxing.

The other important part of this ceremony is that we eat the royal tarts here. This is the only time that the tarts are ever eaten, making this ceremony extra special. The tarts are the most delicious things anyone has ever tasted. They are a taste sensation amazing enough TO KILL FOR . . . Some people would completely destroy you just to get a bit. Jake and Finn have been to this ceremony because they delivered the tarts. We needed them to carry the tarts because it's so dangerous to deliver them, and Finn and Jake could fight off all the bad guys who tried to steal them. They were not invited to participate in the back rubs.

I'm also a big fan of science barbecues. I love science almost as much as I love being the ruling princess of the Candy Kingdom! I will sometimes invite several other scientists to come to the Candy Castle and join me for a barbecue in the yard behind the castle. We eat delicious barbecue food – mostly chicken – and listen to brilliant presentations about the world of science. The scientists get to present their recent discoveries, findings, theories and inventions, all while we eat. We all learn a lot and eat a lot, too!

One of the best science experiments that I have ever completed was my meticulous creation of **the universe's most perfect sandwich**. I've included some instructions below, should anyone else want to try to make one too!

INGREDIENTS

CHEESE: Create your cheese by spinning a cow on its side, in a centrifuge. Then, simply slice your cheese to perfection by molecularly unravelling the cheese brick.

LETTUCE: Use edible growth chemicals to expand and then shrink your lettuce leaf to the ideal size. You must then shred the leaf by hitting it like a baseball.

TOMATOES: To create your tomato, teleport a jellyfish and a red balloon together, then karate-chop into three pieces. Add one perfect slice to your sandwich.

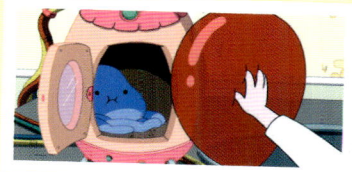

BREAD: Bake your bread from fresh dough, using magic, and then carefully slice with laser beams refracted through crystals.

Finally, put your four ingredients into an anti-gravity machine. Inside, they will join together to create the perfect sandwich. Et voila! Eat and enjoy the greatest sandwich ever created. Simple, yet very delicious!

As you can see, there are plenty of great things going on in the Candy Kingdom. A lot more than the few I've told you about here. I really love living in the Candy Kingdom and being its ruler. I get to do all this fun stuff all the time. It's pretty great!

ICE KINGDOM

RULER: Ice King.

INHABITANTS: Ice King, Snow Golem, Ricardio, Gunter and the penguins.

GEOGRAPHY: The landscape is made up entirely of snow and ice. Nothing else.

CLIMATE: It's cold. Very, very cold.

The Ice Kingdom is the total, complete opposite of the Candy Kingdom. The two kingdoms are really close to each other, but they're completely different. The Candy Kingdom is a warm, friendly, algebraic place. The Ice Kingdom is TERRIBLE! Cold, dark, frozen and completely, totally, one hundred per cent evil. It is the home of that loser the Ice King, and even though he thinks he's a hero, he's actually one of the biggest villains in all of Ooo.

We hate being cold, but we sort of love going to the Ice Kingdom. We love it because that's where we get to fight bad guys the most. If everyone there is wrongteous, we get to prove that we're the righteous ones.

Nothing I like better!

Especially if we get to beat the stuff out of Ice King. That guy bugs us! Sometimes we even get to rescue a princess or two from his icy-cold grip.

The bad thing about the Ice Kingdom is that it's hard to move around there because everything is made out of ice so it's really slippery. Sometimes we slip and slide on the ice and look like total idiots.

I hate it when I look like an idiot. I don't mind it when Finn looks like an idiot, though.

We do love beating on some Ice King butt, and there's no question that the best place to do that is the Ice Kingdom. But we still hate being cold and wouldn't ever want to live here.

ICE KING

FOOL! YOUR POWERS ARE NO MATCH FOR MY MAGICAL CROWN!

GUNTER, YOU'RE EMBARRASSING ME!

FINN? UGH! WHY CAN'T YOU EVER BE A PRINCESS?!

NAME:
Ice King (Formerly known as Simon Petrikov).

SPECIES: Wizard.

HOME: Ice Castle.

Biography:

Like a billion years ago, the Ice King was a human named Simon Petrikov. I guess Simon was alive before the Mushroom War. He liked studying antiques (nerd alert!). He found an old crown and put it on. It made him way, way insane and turned him into ice. After the big war, Simon lost all sense of his humanness and became evil. He turned into a banaynays wizard who called himself the Ice King.

He's really annoying. And always up to no good.

We've heard that Simon Petrikov used to have a nice, normal, non-crazy girlfriend called Betty. She left him when he went nuts. He used to call her 'Princess', so that's supposed to be why all the Ice King ever wants to do is kidnap princesses and force them to marry him. We always rescue the princesses and stop Ice King's plans before he can complete them, though.

MORE INFO

It's kind of become routine for us.

CATEGORY: Enemy.

APPEARANCE: Blue skin with a white beard, a yellow crown and blue robes.

ACCESSORIES: His yellow ice-crown that drove him insane and turned him into ice.

PERSONALITY: Cold, angry, evil.

POWERS: With his ice-crown he can control any form of snow or ice, using them as his weapons to do really evil stuff.

LIKES AND DISLIKES: Likes princesses and romance and being cold. Dislikes fire, heat, us.

DO SAY: "I will marry you, Ice King!" (If you're a princess.)

DON'T SAY: "I liked Simon Petrikov better."

NOTABLE PERSON

GUNTER AND THE PENGUINS

Wak wak.

Wak wak, wak wakwak wak?

Waaaaak. Wakwak.

RAD FACTOR 0 RAD FACTOR

NAME: Gunter and the penguins (names include Gundy, Gunder, Gunthy, Goonter, Goonder, Günder and Gunthelina).

SPECIES: Penguin.

HOME: Ice Kingdom.

Biography:

I try not to be too suspicious of my fellow animal creatures in the Land of Ooo, but Gunter is the most evil thing I've ever seen. Nobody knows if Gunter is a boy penguin or a girl penguin. S/he is called 'he' by the Ice King, but s/he had a baby by laying an egg, so who knows.

Let's call Gunter an 'it'.

Gunter looks cute, but it's so evil. With its sweet little face, you think it would be nice, but nope. It does all the Ice King's bidding and even stole the Ice King's demonic wishing eye to overthrow all of the Land of Ooo and become ruler.

So sneaky.

Gunter is also the leader of the other evil penguins. The Ice King loves Gunter best, though, and so he treats Gunter much better than the other penguins. That sounds kinda unfair, but we guess he does a pretty good job of being an evil sidekick.

MORE INFO

CATEGORY: Enemy sidekick.

APPEARANCE: S/he is a small penguin.

ACCESSORIES: Ice King's video game console, which s/he holds for the Ice King when he plays.

PERSONALITY: Quiet, determined, loyal to the Ice King.

POWERS: Smashing bottles and eating weird stuff, like socks.

LIKES AND DISLIKES: Likes serving the Ice King and being a parent to "Kitten". Dislikes the Fire Kingdom.

DO SAY: "Thank you for all your work, Gunter."

DON'T SAY: "You're fat and can't fly."

SNOW GOLEM

RAD FACTOR 6 RAD FACTOR *

NAME:
Snow Golem.

SPECIES:
Snow Golem.

HOME:
Ice Kingdom.

*Even though we've fought him, that was an accident, and he's nice to animals that are his supposed to be his enemies, like the Fire Wolves.

Biography:

We don't know how many snow golems there are. We know one or two of them pretty well. But there might be a million more. They're snow creatures who can build and rebuild themselves, so there might be tons of them or maybe just a couple.

They're different from the rest of the Ice Kingdom because they're not totally evil. They're actually pretty nice and helpful. They don't seem like they enjoy fighting. If you leave them alone, they'll just live quietly and peacefully in their home. But if you don't leave them alone, watch out — they can be pretty dangerous! The Snow Golem we know is kind, though. He made friends with a fire wolf, which almost killed him from the heat. That was pretty nice of him.

MORE INFO

CATEGORY: Friend.

APPEARANCE: A giant monster made of snow and ice.

ACCESSORIES: Anything he can make with snow.

PERSONALITY: Innocent, kindly, but a little bit scared of Jake and Finn.

POWERS: Can make anything, including lost body parts, out of snow.

LIKES AND DISLIKES: Likes his wife. Dislikes the heat.

DO SAY: "You're a good person, Snow Golem."

DON'T SAY: "We hate you!"

We accidentally smashed his head when we were riding a sled once, too, but he rebuilt it.

LANDMARKS

ICE KING'S CASTLE

There aren't really a whole lot of landmarks or important places in the Ice Kingdom. But we're going to tell you all about the Ice King's Castle, because it's pretty much the most interesting thing there.

It'd be kinda rad if it wasn't all evil and stuff.

It started out as a mountain, but Ice [King] [hollowed] out the entire thing and built a castle on [top]. Don't ask us how he did it because we have n[o idea]. It seems impossible. It's really hard to get insi[de the] castle, because the entire outside is covered in slippery ice.

Making it slippery means it's super-hard for heroes to attack your evil castle. We've had to get there all sorts of crazy ways, like flying by balloon! So yeah, I guess it's actually pretty smart of the Ice King to live in a lump of ice.

Totally. Also, there's a strict 'No Trespassing' law in the Ice Kingdom, which is supposed to stop heroes like us. Ice King gets really mad when we break it.

That law is stupid. We're the only people that ever visit him anyway!

The entrance to the Ice King's Castle is a bunch of windows that look like a giant face. It's not welcoming. In fact, it's real angry and mean-looking — just like the Ice King. He doesn't realize that's why no princesses want to marry him, because he's so wrongteous, and his house is wrongteous, too!

One of the amazing things about the castle is that it's kinda like a weapon, not just a building. That's because, if he wants to, the Ice King can control the whole castle and make it move like an evil robot! That's kinda impressive. And kinda scary.

King hollowed
the inside.
idea.
the

King's castle is waaaay huge. Even though
en there to rescue princesses and do other
tical hero stuff, most rooms are a still a
we'll rescue a princess from some different
exactly what the deal is . . . Until then,
w about the Ice King's living space!

The **main room**
has a bed made
of ice. It looks nice
and comfortable (if you're
nuts and like sleeping in the
freezing cold). Weirdly, it also
has a drum kit and a lot of
gym equipment. Actually, that
kind of makes sense because
Ice King is always trying
to impress princesses, and
princesses like rock stars and
guys with big muscles!

The Ice King has a **princess
cage** here too, which is
soooo messed up. I hate
even looking at it. He uses it to keep
princesses in when he kidnaps them and
tries to force them to marry him.

He's got a **kitchen** and a **dining room**, but we don't think Ice King cooks food. There's always a bunch of takeout pizza boxes on his floor. And, if he did cook, his whole castle could melt and then he'd be living in a puddle. He'd be the Puddle King.

The basement of the Ice King's Castle is full of monsters and weapons and technological stuff that he uses to fight us. It's all useless, though, because we're more algebraic than any monster or weapon. He can't even beat us with his icy magic! Hahaha. In your face, Ice King!

Ice King's **Ninja Cave** is a secret chamber where he keeps collectible ninja stuff. And we've heard that he has a room called 'The Past', where he keeps loads of old stuff from his life – even from when he was Simon Petrikov! Crazy.

Finally, there's a room in the Ice King's Castle that holds a **portal** to the Spirit World. Loads of smoke and stuff comes from the portal, and it's in the basement. Because basements are creepy and the Spirit World is creepy. They're the perfect creepy combo.

MAGIC

Some people think that Jake's stretching powers are magical, but they're really not. At all. But magic is real. And it's one of the sweetest, most math things in the whole world; no, the whole UNIVERSE. But there are some important rules to remember if you're gonna use magic. First, you can only use it for good stuff. This is soooo important. If you try to use magic for evil, like the Ice King always does, we will kick your butt. Second, magic takes practice, but the more you practice the better you get at it, and the better you get at it, the more powerful a wizard you can become.

Finn went to wizard school once. He learned all about magic. But they made him take an Oath of Responsibility, so he can't just have fun with his magic, only help people.

Stupid oath. So boring.

We've had some good adventures with magic, like heroically saving our friends and even the whole world from evil wizards. But we've also had some problems with magic. Not everybody follows their Oath of Responsibility. When some guys get brainwashed by magic, or turned into a streetlight or whatever, then we have to figure out a way to free them from the evil spell they're under. That can be tough sometimes. So, just use your magic for good, so you don't hurt anybody, pal.

We'll come get you if you use magic for evil. That's a promise!

Just try to use it mostly for good. But we won't tell anyone if you use it for a little mischief now and then. It can be kinda fun.

A LOT of fun.

BEING HEROIC

People ask us all the time what it means to be a hero. We're the most awesome heroes in the world, so we totally know what it means to be heroic. Being heroic doesn't mean that you're famous or that you have a fan club or that you're someone's super-smooth idol. That might happen if you're heroic, but that's not exactly what it means. Being heroic means that you always do the right thing for the right reason.

The right reason?

Yeah, you know, like saving a princess from the Ice King, and not expecting a big reward or anything. Just doing it because it's the rad thing to do.

Oh. Yeah. We don't care about rewards. At all.

We like saving people because it's fun, too. It takes courage to be heroic. Sometimes the most heroic thing you can do is save yourself by facing your fears. Like when Finn faced his fear of the ocean. That was pretty heroic, dude.

Yeah, well, I wasn't even that scared, bro. I totally kept cool about it.

Relax, man. I'm just saying that you do heroic stuff all the time.

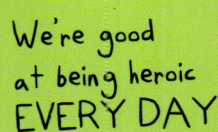

We're good at being heroic EVERY DAY. Like when we rescue people or fight monsters, or wha-ever. All it takes to be a hero is courage and honesty and doing the right thing at the right time in the right place for the right reason. I guess that's why they call it being 'righteous!'

REMEMBER THE TIME?

We've fought a lot of mathematical battles in the Ice Kingdom. Mostly, they've been when the lame Ice King has lamely captured a princess and tried to force her to marry him. We always righteously storm the castle and break the princesses free.

Yeah, but remember the time you had a dream about the Flame Princess and Ice King fighting, but woke up before you saw who the winner was? So you manipulated them both so they would actually fight in real life?

Ah, nuts. Don't go there, man.

We've got to go there, Finn. It's important to the history of the Ice Kingdom, because it made the Ice Kingdom history. So, Finn took Flame Princess on a picnic in the Ice Kingdom, where they saw the Ice King carrying home some groceries. Finn made Flame Princess think the Ice King was making fun of her and that made her mad, so she attacked the Ice King. The battle was crazy brutal. They both used their special abilities – fire and ice – to attack each other. It was intense. But they stopped fighting after a little while, so Finn wrote letters pretending to be each ruler and sent them to the other. They were way, way insulting so Flame Princess and Ice King met for another showdown. The fighting grew so intense that Flame Princess destroyed the whole Ice Kingdom.

I rescued Gunter and the Ice King, so that was good. They were rebuilding the Ice King's castle in no time!

Yeah, that's good. But Flame Princess found out you'd tricked her and totally dumped you.

Yeah. I felt bad that the Ice Kingdom got destroyed but I'm so over Flame Princess. We weren't meant to be.

I always thought it was weird that you two were together in the first place. And now you're responsible for the destruction of an entire kingdom.

I know, dude. But I've apologized a million times for that. It's all good now.

BONUS ENCOUNTERS

With the Ice Kingdom being kinda destroyed, seeing the Ice King and Gunter is difficult enough, but it's even harder to meet the other former residents. If you do happen to see them, though, go ahead and put a check mark in the box next to their picture, pal.

ICECLOPS ☐

This big blue giant guy hangs out in the fields of snow surrounding the Ice Kingdom. He's a cyclops, which means he has only one eye. He wears clothes made of snow and is usually having tons of fun smiling and playing in the snow and ice. Dude knows how to have a good time.

KITTEN ☐

Kitten is Gunter's child. That must suck for her. She's kind of like a weird little cat that can float and has laser vision. She's been known to help Gunter and the penguins when they've gone into battle or faced enemies in the Ice Castle. Like us.

ICE-O-PEDE ☐

The Ice-O-Pede is a giant insect-like creature with a bunch of legs, and it's made out of ice. It has lasers on its back and Ice King used it as an assault vehicle one time. It's got a gross pincer mouth and a rock-hard body so it's a totally dangerous weapon. The only way we've been able to kick its butt is by throwing poisoned pies at it until it collapses and dies. But that takes a lot of work. We don't know how many Ice-O-Pedes there are. We've only seen one. But there might be more!

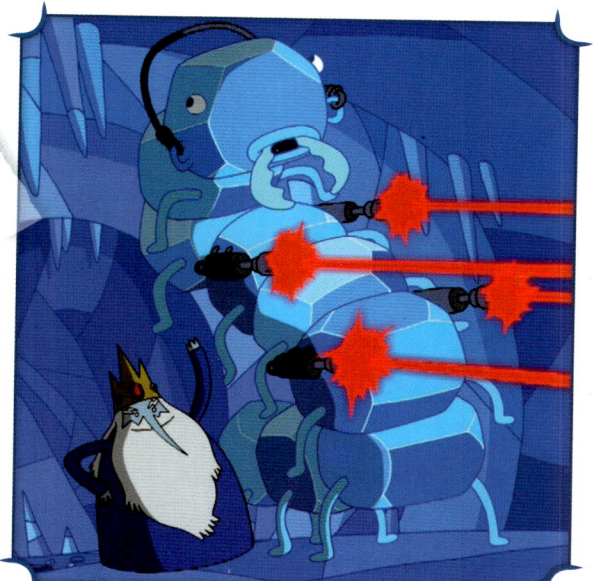

Ice King's Guide to Finding a Wife

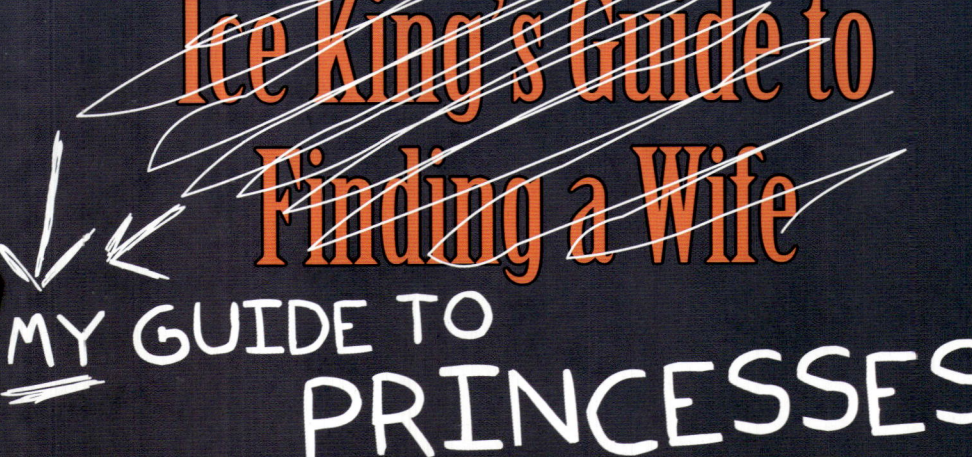

MY GUIDE TO PRINCESSES

Finn and Jake have been telling lots of lies about me in this book. Silly little fools! I paid for these pages so I can tell my side of the story. I'm not actually obsessed with marrying princesses. The marriage laws in the Ice Kingdom are way too complicated for me to always want to get married. You have to tie up the bride and stuff like that. It's too much work. I'm not married because I haven't found the right bride. Honest! Don't you believe me?!

Here are all the princesses and why I refuse to marry them.

Yeah, right. They refuse to marry you.

PRINCESS BUBBLEGUM

Too sticky. You know how hard it is to get gum out of a beard? Besides, we have way too much kidnapping history.

BEE PRINCESS

Don't want to get stung.

BOUNCE HOUSE PRINCESS

Stopped me from meeting princesses at the princess party.

BREAKFAST PRINCESS

I don't like toast.

COTTON CANDY PRINCESS

Too short.

ELBOW PRINCESS

I like her, but after I stole her hips, I felt like she hated me.

EMBRYO PRINCESS

Too young.

EMERALD PRINCESS

She liked the Nice King too much.

ENGAGEMENT RING PRINCESS

Too desperate. I don't want someone who's desperate!

FLAME PRINCESS

She's my mortal enemy.

GHOST PRINCESS

Too ghosty.

HOT DOG PRINCESS

She freed Jake when I held him prisoner… I mean… when he was a guest in my home.

JUNGLE PRINCESS

She has a skull on her head. That scares me.

LAUREL PRINCESS

I saw her in the Imagination Zone. That means no deal.

LIZARD PRINCESS

Same problem. Imagination Zone. Can't do it.

LUMPY SPACE PRINCESS

It's me, not you, dear.

MUSCLE PRINCESS

Too buff. But I did use her left arm for my Princess Monster Wife.

OLD LADY PRINCESS

Tried this one. It just didn't work out.

ORANGE PRINCESS

Can't see her face, so she's not the one.

PEANUT PRINCESS

I think I'm allergic to peanuts.

PRINCESS BEAUTIFUL

She died. Of baldness.

PRINCESS MONSTER WIFE

This princess came as close to perfection as possible. I made her from parts of all the other princesses and we were happy together. Until she realized how I'd made her, and returned all the body parts I'd stolen to their rightful owners.

PRINCESS PRINCESS PRINCESS

Too many heads. It's gross.

PURPLE PRINCESS

I met her as the Nice King. I didn't like her.

RAGGEDY PRINCESS

Don't need someone who can sew.

SKELETON PRINCESS

Bites too much.

SLIME PRINCESS

Too slimy.

SPACE ANGEL PRINCESS

I don't want to live in space.

TOAST PRINCESS

I already said, I don't like toast. Besides, she's the sister of Breakfast Princess, and I didn't want to start a family fued.

TURTLE PRINCESS

She's a librarian. Booorrriiinnggg.

WILDBERRY PRINCESS

Too fragile.

Ice King, you're a liar. You want to marry any or all of these princesses. You aren't fooling anyone! If any single one of these princesses told you she'd marry you, you'd do it in a second.

I KNOW! ARGGGGH... I JUST WANT TO MARRY A PRINCESS SO BAD!

My Fan Fiction

(a.k.a. Imaginary and Excellent Gender-Swapped Versions of Various Existing Peeps)

HELLO AGAIN! I've bought up some extra pages to share a sample of my mind-blowing fan fiction with you. It's incredibly good. Ask anyone who's heard it - they'll all tell you it's the best and anyway, I'll freeze those who disagree. Read my cool character bios and decide for yourselves if I am supremely talented!! (Hint: I am! Fools.)

Introducing Fionna

Ice Queen, why are you always predatoring on dudes?

Come on, you heard what he said. I'm, like, his guy friend.

I can't believe I fell for this trash! You got me to show up in a dress and a purse. . . my purse! My sword!

NAME: FIONNA.
SPECIES: Human.

BIOGRAPHY

If only Fionna the Human Girl was real, I would marry that feisty female in a heartbeat. If she existed outside of my imagination, she would consider me the hottest hottie. I know this for a fact, because I made her up! With knee-length golden hair, an adorable blue outfit and hip athletic socks, Fionna is a reeeeal cutie.

Fionna tries to stay cool, but gets angry when she's being defeated by the majestic Ice Queen. Which is all the time. She enjoys trying to rescue princes (mostly the insipid Gumball) with swordplay and other silliness. She hates it when boys think she's in love with them, because she secretly wants to marry a supremely attractive, powerful king with magical icy powers. We are a rare, sought-after breed.

ICE-COOL **8** FACTOR

MORE INFO

CATEGORY: Imaginary but delightful female.

APPEARANCE: Human with super-crazy-long blonde hair. White hat, long knee-high socks.

ACCESSORIES: White rabbit hat (not a bear hat - that would be stupid), crystal sword.

PERSONALITY: Brave but ultimately inferior to Ice Queen. Anyway, who cares when she looks so cute?!

POWERS: No special powers, except awesome amounts of fearlessness.

LIKES AND DISLIKES: Likes going on adventures and rescuing dudes in distress. Dislikes being bamboozled by Ice Queen.

DO SAY: "Let's rescue the prince!"

DON'T SAY: "Admit it, you're in love with me."

Introducing Cake

NAME: CAKE.

SPECIES: Magical Cat.

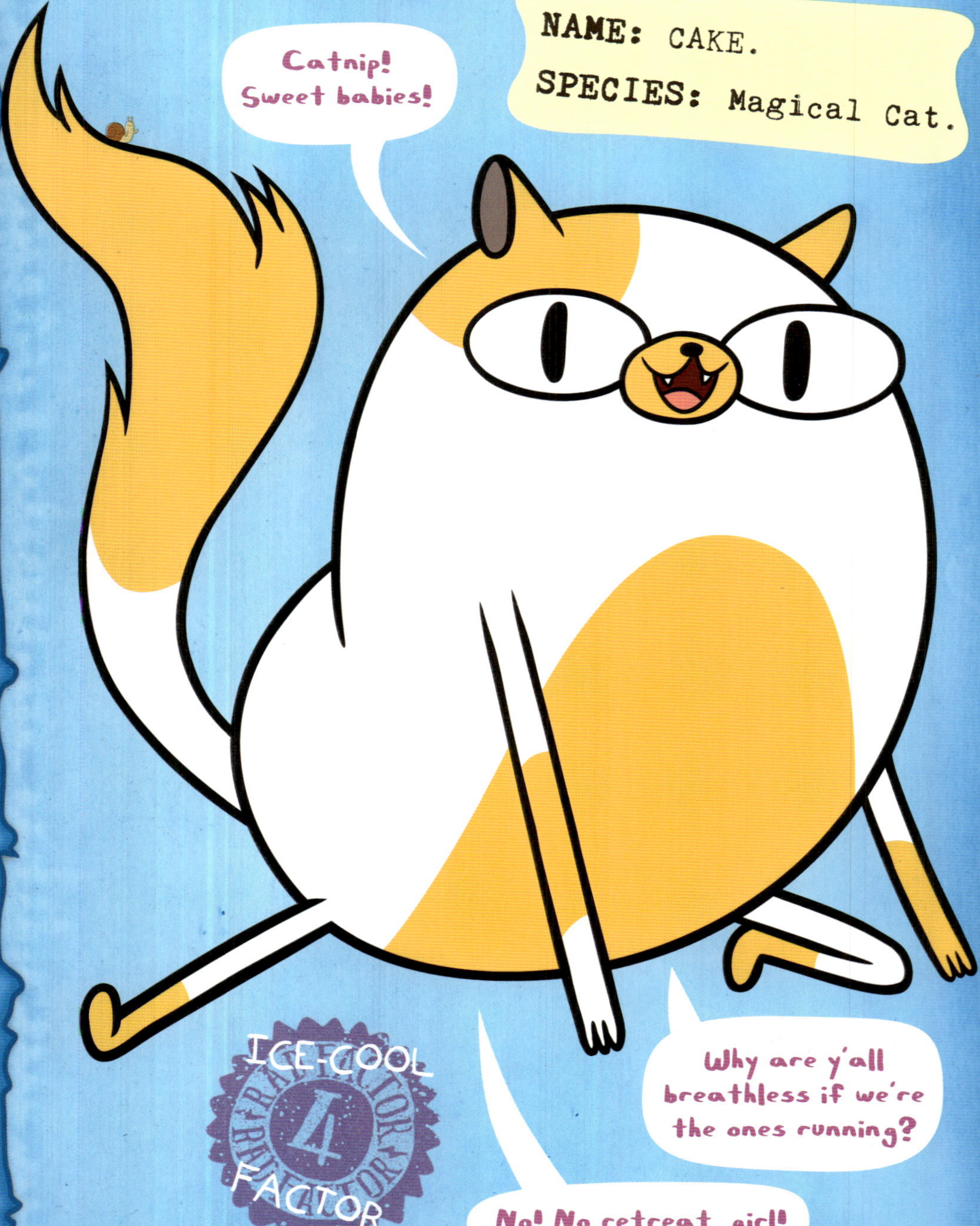

BIOGRAPHY

Lemme tell you about Fionna's adopted big sister, Cake. I don't even know how Fionna puts up with this annoying ball of fluff! She's irritating to speak to due to her relentless sassiness and constant mentions of her tail frizz. And she plays the dulcimer, which is a super-lame instrument - even lamer than a viola. Ok, so she has magical stretching powers and can see in the dark (because she's a cat, duh). But let's be real - she's still no match for the Ice Queen. BECAUSE NOBODY IS!!

All Cake ever really does is boss Fionna around, giving her worthless advice, especially about boys and romance. Pfft. She does this because she's "in love" or whatever with her boyfriend, Lord Monochromicorn. He is way too cool for her and obviously would much prefer to be hitched to the Ice Queen, anyway. That gorgeous icy monarch can't control her sheer animal magnetism!!

MORE INFO

CATEGORY: Imaginary Cat.

APPEARANCE: White cat with giant eyes and light-coloured spots.

ACCESSORIES: She's got a fluffy tail that can sense evil, and claws for climbing mountains and stuff.

PERSONALITY: Too sassy. Annoyingly protective of her family and friends.

POWERS: Can stretch her body into almost any shape and can see in the dark. (Her creepy cat eyes change colour when she does this.)

LIKES AND DISLIKES: Likes catnip, Fionna and Lord Monochromicorn. Dislikes the Ice Queen, because the Ice Queen could so easily steal Cake's boyfriend.

DO SAY: "Hey!" (Especially if you're Lord Monochromicorn.)

DON'T SAY: "I'm going to capture Fionna!"

Introducing Prince Gumball

> Wow, Fionna. You're, you're just really incredible. Maybe we should meet up, for a date?

NAME: PRINCE GUMBALL.

SPECIES: Candy Person.

ICE-COOL FACTOR 5

BIOGRAPHY

Sappy pink prince, most notable for being captured by the Ice Queen a load of times. The best was when Her Majesty hung him upside-down in a big ice-block from the ceiling of his own bedroom! Hahaha. FOOL.

Gumball enjoys baking, which is like doing science experiments, except cooler. He is pals with Fionna the Human, but deep down, Gumball is probably 100% in love with Ice Queen (because why wouldn't he be?).

MORE INFO

APPEARANCE: Pink skin, pink hair, pink everything. With puffy sleeves.

LIKES AND DISLIKES: Likes baking, dislikes being captured by Ice Queen (but actually secretly enjoys it).

DO SAY: "Let's bake cream puffs!"

DON'T SAY: "Wanna hang at the Biennial Gumball Ball? Get it, HANG?! Hahaha."

Introducing Marshall Lee

NAME:
MARSHALL LEE.

SPECIES:
Vampire.

Did you think I was lying? I said I'm evil, without even trying!

BIOGRAPHY

Ooh, Marshall Lee is one moody vampiric hipster dude. I mean, I invented him, so he's only as moody as I make him, but WHATEVER. He's been a teenager for thousands of years so that's why he's all angsty.

Marshall has sick evil powers, like being able to raise the dead and transform into a bat, all while keeping his swishy black hair intact. He's also a musician who raps and plays electric guitar. Man, this guy is soooo cool.

ICE-COOL **8** FACTOR

MORE INFO

APPEARANCE: Trendy clothes, gothy hair, permanent bite marks to neck.

LIKES AND DISLIKES: Likes devouring the colour red. Dislikes anyone questioning his bad villain status.

DO SAY: "You're a bad rockin' dude and an awesome rapper."

DON'T SAY: "You're a big ol' plaid-smothered softie!"

Introducing Lord Monochromicorn

NAME: LORD MONOCHROMICORN.

SPECIES: Monochromicorn.

BIOGRAPHY

Thundery, blacker-than-black flying steed. Only able to communicate in Morse Code by tapping his hooves, like a c-c-c-cool, charcoal-covered Lord of the Dance. Yeah.

Lord Monochromicorn is BFFs with Prince Gumball, who calls him 'Mo-Chro', because that's the cool kind of bro name that bros use. He is romantically involved with Cake, although I might meddle with this in a future edition of my fan fic because Cake has a bad 'tude.

Morse code:

.... .-.--

English translation:
'Hey.'

ICE-COOL
RARITY FACTOR
7
FACTOR

MORE INFO

APPEARANCE: Black with silvery mane and intense white eyes.

LIKES AND DISLIKES: Likes running around with Prince Gumball. Too cool to dislike anything.

DO SAY: "Hey, gorgeous!" (If you're Cake.)

DON'T SAY: Anything not in Morse Code.

Introducing Ice Queen

NAME: ICE QUEEN.

SPECIES: Witch (formerly a water nymph).

The prince shall be mine!

BIOGRAPHY

I totally saved the best 'til last - yes, it's ICE QUEEN!! She's a bad babe with magnificent icy powers, not to mention luscious, luminous white hair and stunning taste in blue ball gowns.

Even though Ice Queen likes to capture Prince Gumball, she's actually way out of his league. She should be with someone as scheming, merciless and ice-tastic as she is . . . someone like ME!! ICE KING! POW!!! Ah, Ice Queen, if only you existed outside of my imagination.

ICE-COOL 10000 FACTOR

MORE INFO

APPEARANCE: Bejewelled, blue and b-e-a-uuutiful.

LIKES AND DISLIKES: Likes reigning supreme, dislikes anyone standing between her and her prince.

DO SAY: "I bow down before you, oh stunning Queen!"

DON'T SAY: "Take off that tiara!"

MOUNTAIN KINGDOM

I've lived in places all over Ooo, including Finn and Jake's Tree Fort!

RULER: Marceline, we guess?

INHABITANTS: Marceline and Schwable.

GEOGRAPHY: Mountainous and cavernous. (That means lots of caves.)

CLIMATE: Cold and mountain-y.

On the outskirts of the Candy Kingdom is the Mountain Kingdom. It's . . . a lot of mountains. Those mountains have a lot of caves. And not really very many people live there. It's pretty ugly. You know: cold, damp, high up. Really everything you'd expect from a kingdom in the mountains. It's probably cold because it's really close to the Ice Kingdom, too.

It doesn't seem like they have a princess or a prince or an earl or a king or anyone ruling this kingdom. Pretty much the only person we know who lives there is Marceline and her zombie dog, Schwable. It's a pretty good place for them to live since Marceline's a vampire and her dog's a zombie. Those kind of people like living in terrible places.

We don't go to the Mountain Kingdom very much. We don't really have adventures there. Nobody is ever there to fight. Or to rescue. Or to discover. The place is boring. And ugly. Thinking about it makes Finn kinda mad.

So mad. I need to go and destroy some evil just to chill!

Relax, Finn. Don't let the mountains make you crazy. They're fine.

MARCELINE
(AND SCHWABLE)

So, Finn, I need you to strangle some pixies.

Vampires can't beat ghosts. It's like a rock-paper-scissors thing.

Ha! Looks like you're not as perfect as you thought. Guess you can't judge me anymore.

RAD FACTOR 8 RAD FACTOR

NAME: Marceline Abadeer, the Vampire Queen (and Schwable the Zombie Dog).

SPECIES: Vampire and Zombie Dog.

HOME: Mountain Kingdom Caves.

Biography:

Marceline used to be a human. We guess she was alive before the Mushroom War and got bit some time by a vampire and got turned into one. She's, like, a thousand years old, but she acts like she's eighteen or nineteen. She's a kick-butt bass player and she loves to party. We like it when she parties and invites us to party with her, because those parties can be fun. Except for when Marceline decides to transform into some sort of terrifying monster. Then, not so much.

She hangs out with her zombie dog, Schwable, kinda like how I hang out with a living dog, Jake.

Don't go comparing zombie dogs to regular dogs, pal. We're totally not the same thing. Schwable's OK, I guess, and I dig Marceline. But we're not the same, just like vampires and humans are different.

MORE INFO

CATEGORY: Friend.

APPEARANCE: A pale-skinned vampire with long black hair. Dresses like a rock star. Has more clothes than anyone else in the Land of Ooo. Seriously, every time we see her she's wearing something totally different.

ACCESSORIES: She never leaves home without her axe-shaped bass guitar.

PERSONALITY: Rock star, mischievous, aggressive, a little sentimental.

POWERS: Shape-shifting, floating, lights fires with her mind, raises the dead, expert bass player.

LIKES AND DISLIKES: Likes rockin' out, red food, nighttime. Dislikes sunlight, mirrors.

DO SAY: "Let's rock, Marceline!"

DON'T SAY: "Let's hang out with your dad."

MARCELINE'S CAVE

Marceline's cave is the weirdest place in the Mountain Kingdom, because it's nothing like you'd expect. She lives in a cave, yeah, but in her cave is a house. A real house. Like, with a front door and picket fence.

> Pretty weird. Why would anyone live in a house? I mean, candy castles, tree forts, Lumpy Space, sure. But a house?

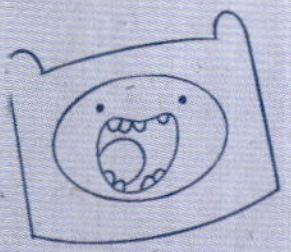

She keeps it all decorated nice and stuff, too. She even has plants that she grows there. Well, we guess she has this zombie gardener dude who actually grows and takes care of the plants. The plants are alive, but everyone and everything else there is undead.

Maybe she wants to live in a house because she lived in one before the Mushroom War. We don't get what all the stuff she has in her house is, but it's stuff that makes her happy, and happy Marceline is much better than sad Marceline or, worse, angry Marceline who turns into crazy monsters and freaks me out! At home, Marceline can play basketball or suck all the red colour out of her furniture. No big deal. It's just like how we can have all our awesome trophies and stuff in the basement of our house. She probably doesn't get how awesome that is!

Hang on, our trophies are awesome. But keeping a load of old human stuff isn't. It's weird and kind of creepy. But I guess that's how we could describe Marceline – weird and kind of creepy.

But still a radical dame.

Oh, Schwable lives there, too. If you're gonna have a zombie dog, you gotta have a good home for her. Jake should know. As a real-life, living, non-zombie dog, he needs a good home. So we guess Marceline's house must be perfect for her . . . and Schwable.

Even if we think it's a little weird.

ROCKIN' OUT

Yo, Marceline here. Jake and Finn asked me if I wanted to write some stuff for their book or whatever. I said no. But then I changed my mind, because I figured people would benefit from hearing my wise thoughts on important stuff. Like rocking out.

Finn and Jake aren't in a band, so they don't get to rock out, but they are missing out BIG TIME. It's one of the most fun things anyone can do. Playing my axe bass and singing makes me feel less like I wanna raise an army of the dead – which has to be a good thing, right?

I'm gonna tell you a big secret about rocking out right now – you know what it is? You don't have to have a kick-butt bass guitar to rock out with the pros. You can rock out with regular stuff you have around the house. You can play the drums on anything, like garbage cans, or cooking pans. All you need is something big and empty and something to hit it with, and all of a sudden, it's like you're playing a real drum kit. Just hit 'em hard and fast.

Another important part of rocking out is head-banging. You bounce your head up and down real quick.

Yeah. And you got to look the part, too. Marceline - tell them what a rockin' vampire queen should look like.

I've got a million outfits that look like rock star clothes. Lots of stuff in red, black and dark, moody colours. Torn jeans, dresses, tank tops, boots, big belts. It's all pretty punk rock. Basically, if your parents don't want you to wear it, it's the perfect outfit for being a rock star and rocking out.

ADVENTUROUS ADVICE

ROCKIN' LYRICS

Some people think that singing songs is lame. If you're not a great singer, then it can be lame. Especially for the people that can hear you singing. But if you write your own songs, and your own lyrics, then your rocking out will NEVER be lame. For example, I wrote these real deep lyrics about a time when I was mad at Bonnibel (known to you as Princess Bubblegum):

Sorry I don't treat you like a goddess,
Is that what you want me to do?
Sorry I don't treat you like you're perfect,
Like all your little loyal subjects do,
Sorry I'm not made of sugar,
Am I not sweet enough for you?
Is that why you always avoid me?
That must be such an
inconvenience to you.

See, those lyrics have some genuine FEELINGS in them. That's the secret to rocking out - you gotta believe whatever it is that you're singing about. Someone once wrote me a song that made me get emotional. Real emotional. OK, I cried a little bit. DON'T EVER TELL ANYONE THAT! But the reason the song made me sad was that the lyrics were so deep and full of sadness:

Marceline, is it just you and me in the wreckage of the world?

That must be so confusing for a little girl.

And I know you're going to need me here with you.

But I'm losing myself, and I'm afraid you're gonna lose me too.

This magic keeps me alive, but it's making me crazy,

And I need to save you, but who's going to save me?

Please forgive me for whatever I do,

When I don't remember you.

I mean, those words are just so ...so ... Um ... I gotta leave this section here, I think there's something in my eye ...

What's up, kids? Marceline here again. Last time, I promise. Tricks and pranks are the best things in the whole world. Especially if people don't know you're going to do them. I really like messing with people's minds, like making them think they've been turned into a vampire, or that I kidnapped their best friend, or tricking them into being my slave.

She tricked me. Hated it! Worst gig ever!

When they fall for stuff it's totally worth it. But sometimes people get in trouble when they fall for my tricks. Like when I made Finn and Jake think they were vampires and then a butt-load of ghosts tried to hurt them. I hate when that happens because then I end up having to save people. People always screw up my tricks and take all the fun out of them. So it's probably better not to mess too hard with people or else you're going to have to clean up the mess.

Part of being the best prankster in the world is not being scared of anything. I've been chillin' in the Land of Ooo for, like, ten centuries or glob knows how long, and that's made me totally not scared of anything. If you're scared of getting caught, or people being mad at you, you won't be a very good prankster. Take it from me, that's what pranking is all about – fearlessness! That, and having a wicked sense of humour and really loving to mess with your peeps.

It's a big deal to make sure no one gets hurt. Like I said, if you have to clean up a mess because someone didn't react to the trick right or they got hurt or killed, that's the worst. So, be careful, I guess. But have fun. And mess them up in the head!

REMEMBER THE TIME?

Marceline is a good friend and we've had some good times with her. Like, remember that time when we first met her and she came over to our house and tried to kick us out because it was her house first? And she pretended to kill you?

Yeah . . . I remember. It's not fun to be pretend-killed by a vampire chick that wants to steal your house. And she totally messed with you, too, when she made you her henchman. But I saved you, buddy, by knocking her hat off and making her see the sunlight.

Yeah. . . Saved me.

Her stories are the craziest stuff ever, like how she used to hang out with Ice King when they were both humans during the Mushroom War.

I don't remember that.

Of course you don't. We weren't there. We weren't even alive yet! It was, like, a thousand years ago. But Ice King knew her. She told us. She was a little human kid and he was a weird human adult. He found the ice crown and started going nuts, so he wrote some cheesy love-song apologizing for forgetting her or something (I forget), and they sang it together.

Oh yeah! She also told us about the time she was a kid and Ice King took care of her when she was sick. I'm glad he's never tried to take care of me when I'm sick, because he's crazy, and I wouldn't eat any soup or anything he brought me to make me feel better. He'd probably try to poison me or something sneaky.

Yeah, he'd probably poison you — but that's because if he had to fight you, he knows you'd win! He is sooo lame.

LUMPY SPACE

RULER: Lumpy Space Royal Family.

INHABITANTS: Lumpy People.

GEOGRAPHY: In outer space, vast, cloud-like, lumpy with a dark abyss on its borders.

CLIMATE: As cold and dark as anything in the universe, because it's in outer space.

Lumpy Space is not really the most exciting place in the Land of Ooo, if you can even say it's in the Land of Ooo! It's in outer space, and it's really messed up how you get there. You have to find a frog sitting on a toadstool in the Cotton Candy Forest and give him a secret password, 'Whatevers 2009', and then he snatches you with his tongue, and you travel through his guts (I don't want to think about it) and you're suddenly in Lumpy Space.

It's pretty gross. Frog guts. Yuck.

We've been to Lumpy Space, but we didn't feel too welcome there. The Lumpy Space People are grouchy all the time. They kinda hate everyone who's not lumpy. They call them 'smoothies.'

And they say it like it's a bad thing!

They can also turn regular non-lumpy people into Lumpy Space People if they bite them. We've been bitten in the past and became lumpy for a second. It was so wrongteous. On the plus side, it meant we could float through Lumpy Space real easy.

Lumpy Space is ruled by the Lumpy Space Royal Family, which is Lumpy Space King and Queen, and Lumpy Space Princess. Lumpy Space Princess is actually a good friend of ours. She treats everybody except us and Princess Bubblegum pretty badly and she's generally kind of mean. But, whatever — we have to protect the Lumpy Space Kingdom anyway, because there's this giant Lumpy Space Reactor in the middle of it. If that gets destroyed, then the whole Land of Ooo gets destroyed with it.

LUMPY SPACE PRINCESS

First you should check out my house. It's, like, kinda lame but way less lame than, like, your house.

I know I mess things up sometimes, but I'm really trying! And you guys are supposed to be my friends! Not like the fake ones I have here!

Oh my glob, you guys. . . DRAMA BOMB!

RAD FACTOR 5 RAD FACTOR

NAME: Lumpy Space Princess (nickname 'LSP').

SPECIES: Lumpy Space Person.

HOME: Lumpy Space.

Biography:

Lumpy Space Princess is one of our friends, but she doesn't always treat everyone nice. She gets grouchy and makes fun of people. We think it's because she's from Lumpy Space. If we were from Lumpy Space, we'd be grouchy and mean, too. LSP is really, really, REALLY grouchy, though.

> She even bit me once.

> I think it was an accident. She said it was.

> You just think that because she has a crush on you.

> No. That's weird. We're just friends! Lumpy Space Princess doesn't even really like the Land of Ooo. It's like we're from two different worlds, dude!

Anyway, LSP and her parents, the King and Queen of Lumpy Space, don't really get along. They kicked her out of Lumpy Space for a while, but then they needed us to get her back. When your friends fight with their parents, that's the worst.

> If you ever meet LSP, she'll probably not like you. Especially if you're a smoothie.

MORE INFO

CATEGORY: Friend.

APPEARANCE: Lumpy, purple, like a cloud.

ACCESSORIES: A glowing yellow star on her forehead.

PERSONALITY: Kind of a brat, gossipy, feels entitled to everything, mean to most people (except maybe Finn).

POWERS: Can float (like all Lumpy Space People), can turn smoothies into Lumpy Space People if she bites them.

LIKES AND DISLIKES: Likes Finn and Princess Bubblegum. Dislikes most other people.

DO SAY: "I love Lumpy Space People!"

DON'T SAY: "You should be exiled to the Candy Kingdom."

LUMPY SPACE KING AND QUEEN

RAD FACTOR **4** RAD FACTOR

> What did you just say?

> You've made your mother cry for the last time, Daughter! You are hereby banned from using the royal car!

> Daughter! Have you brought smooth people into our domain?!

NAME: Lumpy Space King and Queen (nickname 'Boobly Bear').

SPECIES: Lumpy Space People.

HOME: Lumpy Space.

Biography:

The Lumpy Space King and Queen look like they're one person with two heads, but they're not. They're a married couple in Lumpy Space. Which means they have to actually be, like, physically attached to each other.

Totally weird. And then when they were married, they had a kid. That's Lumpy Space Princess, but they just call her 'Daughter.'

They're pretty annoying. Basically they don't let LSP do anything. So when she wants to do something, she decides to run away or get kicked out of Lumpy Space. We hate when she does that, though, because then her parents make us find her in the Candy Kingdom and bring her back home.

Jake, babe, it's so obvi that I DID NOT need you guys to bring me home.

Oh, sure! You were fine. Living off beans. Totally alone.

Anyway, because the King and Queen are strict parents and also the rulers of a sort-of-kingdom, they're not very nice. We don't really like them. Lumpy Space Princess doesn't really like them either. That probably says a lot about how not nice they are.

MORE INFO

CATEGORY: Rulers.

APPEARANCE: Like most Lumpy Space People, they are large, purple, cloud-like, and lumpy. However, because they're married, they're literally attached to each other.

ACCESSORIES: They both wear crowns to show their royal status. They both have stars on their foreheads and the King has glasses, too.

PERSONALITY: The King is pretty controlling of LSP, while the Queen is kinda quieter.

POWERS: Like all Lumpy Space People, they can float, and if they bite non-Lumpy people, it makes them lumpy.

LIKES AND DISLIKES: Like Lumpy Space People. Dislike when Lumpy Space Princess runs away or gets in other kinds of trouble.

DO SAY: "Yes, your majesty."

DON'T SAY: "No." To anything.

LUMPY SPACE PRINCESS'S HOUSE

If you're ever gonna visit Lumpy Space, there are some things you need to know about travelling while you're there. You need to be able to float or fly because every place is on its own land lump and they're all separated from each other. So you need to fly or float between them to get where you want to go. You also need to watch out for the Lumpy Space Abyss, which is a bottomless pit that can suck you in to your doom if you're not careful. The Abyss is between all the land lumps.

One of the main places to visit if you're there is Lumpy Space Princess's house. It's the house where she and her family all live. It's just a regular house. Not a castle like most royal families live in. It's pretty big, so we guess that counts for something. It's also kind of lopsided, but it's the perfect house for the Lumpy Royal Family. It's all pink and purple and has blue windows.

Lumpy Space Princess doesn't really live there much, because she doesn't like her parents, so often she'll run away or get exiled and leave the house for a while. One time, I found her sleeping under a tree. She's lucky that she doesn't get sucked into the Lumpy Space Abyss every time she tries leaving. Good thing she has friends, like Melissa, who can drive a flying car to help her get away from the house.

We don't go to LSP's house often, because we don't like her parents much and we don't really have any reason to go there, except if we're dragging her home on orders from the Lumpy Space King. But it's probably the best house in Lumpy Space.

That's not really saying much, though.

LANDMARKS

MAKEOUT POINT

Probably the most important place in Lumpy Space is Makeout Point. Not because that's where all the Lumpy Space People go to make out. That's totally gross. It's important because it's the main place to find the Lumps Antidote.

The Lumps Antidote will turn anyone who is lumpy into a smooth, non-lumpy person. It's a white ball thing. We know, it's weird. For the antidote to work, a lumpy person needs to sit on it for a long time. If you were born a Lumpy Space Person, the antidote only works while you sit on it. You look like a smoothie but only for a while. If you got turned in to a lumpy person because you got bit by a Lumpy Space Person, the antidote will return you to your original form.

Yeah, we've had to use it. That was not the most fun adventure we've ever been on.

There are a bunch of Lumpy Space People who hang out at Makeout Point, not because they're smooching, but because they take turns sitting on the lumps antidote. They're Monty, Glasses and Lenny. Monty didn't seem to like us much when we met him. But Lenny is actually a really nice guy and taught me about the Lumps Antidote. Glasses kinda looks like a fish.

They're OK, except that they don't like being Lumpy Space People and wish they were smoothies. Me and Jake think they should just be who they really are. They were born that way. It's nothing to be ashamed of! Just be yourselves, guys. Be proud of being Lumpy Space People! Find some ladies to hang out with at Makeout Point and quit sitting on the lumps antidote already!

GROWING UP

I've always thought that being a grown-up is way harder than being a kid. Especially if you've got kids of your own. You have to feed them, clothe them, help them understand stuff like danger and adventures. Everybody expects you to be perfect at everything you do, and if you aren't, they get mad at you.

Yeah, right! Being a kid is way worse.

Wrong. Being a grown-up is the worst. No question.

I think that when you're a kid, everybody tells you what to do, and if you don't listen you get grounded or exiled to the Candy Kingdom, or something like that! AND everybody still expects you to be perfect and gets mad when you're not, even if you're just learning something. I know, know, KNOW that being a grown-up is way better than being a kid. Plus, grown-ups don't have to go to school or do homework anymore!

Mind you, a little school never hurt anyone. Actually school is pretty good because it helps people get ready to be a grown-up by teaching you all the stuff you need to know. And then you can teach your kids all that stuff.

You didn't really teach your kids anything, though.

Nah, that's true. They were born super-smart, like little grown-ups. It was weird. But I guess that's what you get when your mom is a Rainicorn.

I guess that being a kid and being a grown-up are both pretty sweet. Either way, you're alive, which means you can go adventuring!

Yeah. You're alive. And that's pretty bombastic!

BEST UNKLE

REMEMBER THE TIME?

So Jake and I have been to Lumpy Space a few times. The first time we went there was when Lumpy Space Princess went nutso and bit Jake at Princess Bubblegum's Marshmallow Tea Party! We had to go to Lumpy Space to get the antidote for the lumps before sunset or Jake would've been a Lumpy Space Person forever and EVER. We were victorious, even if we did make Lumpy Space King mad by even going to Lumpy Space at all. But a bro's got to do what a bro's got to do to save his bro from becoming a Lumpy Space Person!

Yup! I'm glad I'm still me. Remember the time when we went on an adventure to Lumpy Space, because we had to drag LSP back to her house, because she'd run away after having a fight with her folks? It seems like that happens a lot, but maybe it was only the once . . . Anyway, we had to fight LSP first, because she was being a monster and scaring villagers. I don't like monsters scaring villagers, so I'll fight that every time.

That wasn't even the most annoying thing LSP has ever done to us, though. This one time, she pretended to be our 'secretary.' What the what?! Like we'd need a secretary! But she followed us around everywhere. She tried carrying rocks that we were using on an adventure to destroy some magic mirrors that created evil versions of people.

She thought that ALL the mirror-Finns were attracted to her.

NO WAY. Not even Mirror-me would be attracted to her. It was so annoying. She didn't even really want to be our secretary. She was just following us around because she was writing a book on how to attract guys. It didn't work, but the book got published anyway. Total fail.

BONUS ENCOUNTERS
Brad, Melissa and Monty

MELISSA AND BRAD ☐

Melissa and Brad are two teenagers in Lumpy Space that are dating each other. Melissa is Lumpy Space Princess's best friend, and Brad is Lumpy Space Princess's ex-boyfriend, so it's kinda awkward when they all get together.

Finn, I don't even care who Brad dates anymore! I'm, like, totally over him!

Ugh, OK, I take that back. It's not awkward at all. Melissa and Brad don't really hang out with anyone else, but sometimes we see them when we go to Lumpy Space. They never go on adventures with us. But that's ok, because they'd be pretty useless on an adventure. Melissa does have a car, and that's useful sometimes, I guess.

It's kind of funny when Melissa teases LSP about dating her ex-boyfriend. Lumpy Space Princess doesn't seem to mind, but I think deep down it drives her nuts that she's not with Brad anymore, even though SHE dumped HIM.

I don't care. They can have whatever love triangle they want, as long as it doesn't involve me in a love rectangle.

Whatevers, Finn. You WISH you were involved.

Earlier we talked about Monty, Lenny and Glasses because they hang out together at Makeout Point, sitting on the Lumps Antidote all the time. You might or might not actually see them there, because we think they probably have lives and go home sometimes. The most interesting of these three dudes is Monty. If you do see him, put a tick mark in the box below.

MONTY ☐

For a pink Lumpy Space Person, Monty actually looks pretty smooth. It might be because he sits on the antidote a lot. He's with Lenny and Glasses all the time because somebody ditched them at Makeout Point. Monty isn't very trusting of people. When people are nice to him, he thinks it's because they want something and not because they actually like him. It's kinda sad.

LUMPY SPACE PRINCESS'S GUIDE TO PROMCOMING

I guess I'm supposed to tell you about Promcoming. I don't know why. It's not like it's all that great. Actually, I'm just kidding. It's, like, the GREATEST thing in the history of EVER! I'm surprised you've never heard of it. What? You HAVE heard of it? Then what am I telling you for? Oh, probably because you want to know more about it. Well, I know more about it. I know EVERYTHING about it! It's a dance. But it's not JUST a dance. It's like the biggest, greatest, most fun dance ever. And it's always totally FRESH because it happens every single week!

Promcoming is held on its own land lump and people come from all over Lumpy Space to dance and party. Finn and Jake even came once. That was mega awkward. But I guess it proves that Promcoming is the coolest thing ever. Sometimes Lumpy Space People can't get to Promcoming because they get sucked into the Abyss, but that's totally their loss. The best people go every week, like me and my BFF, Melissa. Melissa usually brings her boyfriend, Brad. He's my ex. I like it when he comes because I get to show him what he's missing by not being with me. OH YEAH!

The dance is meant to be for everyone in Lumpy Space. But, whatevs – it's really all about me. I'm the Lumpy Space Princess, but I'm, like, totes the Promcoming Queen every week. No one can dance better than me. No one looks better than me at Promcoming. And no one goes to Promcoming more than me. Other people have fun. That's fine. Just so long as they don't have more fun than me. But that would be totally impossible because I always have the most fun at Promcoming! If you're ever in Lumpy Space you should totally come. Make sure you say hi to me if you do. I might not say hi back though, because I don't know you.

If you do ever come to Lumpy Space and want to go to Promcoming, there's some stuff you should probably know first.

Like, the dress code. It's not formal but it's not casual. It's really just lump. You know, like totally lumpy. If you can't make that work for you, babe, don't bother showing up. It's totally go lump or go home. You won't be better dressed than me, of course, but you should really put some effort into looking your lumpiest. Jake and Finn tried to look their lumpiest when they came to Promcoming, but they actually looked terrible. It was a good thing the Lump Antidote just happened to be there so they could give up their sad attempt to look all lump.

Second, if you're going to try to hit up Promcoming, you need to find someone with a car to get you there. My BFF Melissa has a car, and she drives me like every week. If you don't have a car, you can try floating, but you'll probably get sucked into the Lumpy Space Abyss and never be seen again. Unless you're, like, great at floating, but since you're probably not from around here, I'm guessing you'll totally suck at it.

Third, you better have some kick-butt dance moves, babe, and you better be ready to leave it all on the dance floor. Promcoming brings out THE best dancers in all of Lumpy Space. These guys are serious and you'll look like an idiot if you don't got the moves.

Finally, you better not try to dance with me unless I think you're HOT. How will you know if I think you're hot? Don't worry – I'll totes let you know. Then you'd better dance with me, or I'll be mad. And you wouldn't like me if I was mad.

SO, THAT'S PROMCOMING. SHOW UP. DANCE. LOOK FRESH. IT'S EVERY WEEK AND IT'S THE BEST!

FIRE KINGDOM

RULER: Flame King.

INHABITANTS: The Fire People, Flame Princess, Fire Count.

GEOGRAPHY: Molten lava rivers, lava rock, volcanoes.

CLIMATE: Hotter than anything you've ever experienced.

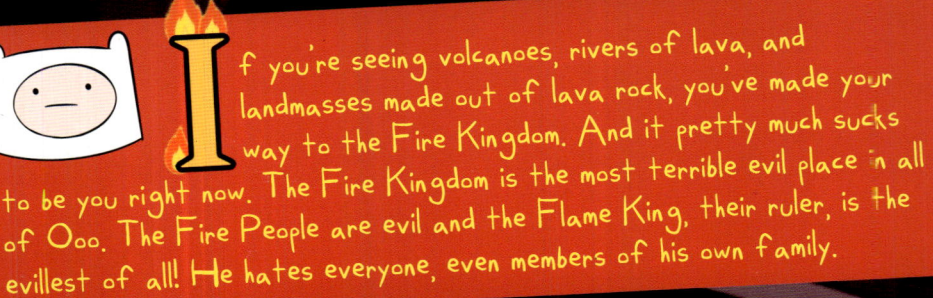

If you're seeing volcanoes, rivers of lava, and landmasses made out of lava rock, you've made your way to the Fire Kingdom. And it pretty much sucks to be you right now. The Fire Kingdom is the most terrible evil place in all of Ooo. The Fire People are evil and the Flame King, their ruler, is the evillest of all! He hates everyone, even members of his own family.

The Ice Kingdom and the Fire Kingdom border each other, and me and Finn think it would be really cool if they started fighting. If that happened, the Snow Beings from the Ice Kingdom would get all melty and turn into water, which would extinguish the Fire People! Round that area of the coast of Ooo is the Isle of Steam, too. Nobody knows if the Isle belongs to the Ice Kingdom or the Fire Kingdom or if it's neutral or something. But it totally makes sense that Steam appears somewhere between Ice and Fire!

Seriously, dudes, if you're already in the Fire Kingdom, get out of there as fast as you can! If you've never been there, don't go there. The place is hot. Super hot. Boiling hot. Volcano hot. The people are all made of fire. The buildings and stuff are all made of fire, too. If you go there and stay too long you will get burned. Or at least sweat a ton. And that's gross. It makes you smell bad.

Except for me. I never sweat.

Hey. Buddy. I've been on plenty of adventures with you and TRUST ME – you've smelled plenty bad. Gross, gross, GROSS.

FLAME PRINCESS

Huh? Why do you torment me? Enough! You should not toy with the emotions of a fire elemental.

You guys are full of magic air.

Do we need a torch? I'm sort of made of fire.

RAD FACTOR 8 RAD FACTOR

NAME:
Flame Princess.

SPECIES:
Fire Person.

HOMES:
Fire Kingdom, Candy Kingdom.

Biography:

Flame Princess and Finn go way back. They dated on and off for a while. She gets mad at Finn a lot. It's because she's so passionate. And she should be. She's a fire elemental, which means she can control flames. She has some serious issues with her dad because he used to keep her trapped in a lantern. He didn't want her going out with her friends, or boys, or anything. Ever.

Talk about mega over-protective!

She escaped to the Candy Kingdom, but things always get kind of messed up when Flame Princess explores new places, because she usually accidentally sets stuff on fire.

We also like her because she likes to fight. That's what we need when we go on adventures — princesses who aren't afraid to go to battle and kick bad guy butt, or torch it.

Plus, she doesn't get mad at me very much.

MORE INFO

CATEGORY: Used to be Finn's girlfriend.

APPEARANCE: Flame Princess is, like all Fire People, made of fire. She wears a fire dress and is all orange, red and yellow — the colours of a flame.

ACCESSORIES: She has a couple of jewels that she wears on her dress and her forehead.

PERSONALITY: Aggressive, passionate, impulsive.

POWERS: Can control fire and use Fire People as weapons.

LIKES AND DISLIKES: Likes Finn (sometimes), fire and battles. Dislikes Finn (sometimes) and water.

DO SAY: "You're hot."

DON'T SAY: "Would you like a glass of water?"

Biography:

You know the Fire Kingdom is really evil? Well, like every kingdom or group of people who follow their leader and act like them, the Fire People and the Fire Kingdom are completely evil because their king is. Seriously, he has, like, no redeeming qualities. He trapped his daughter in a lantern to 'protect' her. He wants to destroy everyone and everything. When his jester was killed, he was kind of happy about it. I mean, a jester! I know clowns can be creepy, but hating on your own jester? Evil, man. Evil.

He totally knows he's evil, too. He's proud of it! He became king by extinguishing his brother. We'd say that was cold, which it was, but since he's made of fire, calling him cold seems completely wrong. But killing your brother so you can be king is wronger, so maybe we WILL call him cold.

We also don't like him because he thinks he's better than everyone else just because he's a king. But he's a king of the worst part of the Land of Ooo, so big deal. "Ooohh, I'm so awesome 'cause I'm the Flame King. Everyone bow down and worship me."

You also don't like him because he didn't think you deserved to date Flame Princess unless you killed me. I'm glad you didn't but, really, what a lousy move for a king.

I can hate him for two reasons. You don't even know.

Anyway, the only thing he could do that we would like is fight Ice King. We've always hoped they might destroy each other. It would probably end up being a draw, so we'd have to keep dealing with them both. We just want them to extinguish and melt each other so there are no more evil kings in the Land of Ooo. That'd be sweet.

MORE INFO

CATEGORY: Enemy.

APPEARANCE:
A gigantic ball of fire.

ACCESSORIES: A suit of armour that protects him from being extinguished.

PERSONALITY: Angry, murderous, pure evil.

POWERS: Can fly very fast as a ball of fire, great agility.

LIKES AND DISLIKES:
Likes evil and power. Dislikes everything else.

DO SAY:
"Yes, your majesty."

DON'T SAY:
"No, your majesty."

FIRE COUNT

ARGGHHHHHH!

I HAVE THE COTTON CANDY PRINCESS!

YOU'LL NEVER DEFEAT ME, BILLY!

NAME: Fire Count.
SPECIES: Fire Person.
HOME: Fire Kingdom.

Biography:

We don't really know very much about the Fire Count except that he lived a way long, long, long, long, long, ong time ago. He was one of the enemies of our hero, Billy, a warrior from a way long, long, long, long, long, long time ago. He was probably the ruler of the Fire Kingdom right after the Mushroom War, when the Land of Ooo was created. He wears a crown hat like Ice King's but it's probably not actually Ice King's. Probably. He liked to kidnap princesses, kind of like Ice King. But he's not actually Ice King, because Ice King was a human named Simon, and Fire Count was always Fire. Probably.

When Billy battled Fire King, it was because Fire Count had kidnapped Cotton Candy Princess. Billy cut him up using his sword. Fire Count was never heard of again. Cotton Candy Princess gave Billy some of her hair. Oh yeah, and then Billy fought a bear.

Billy's mathematical. I can't believe he battled all the bad guys and always won. He's my hero.

Mine too.

Fire Count rots.

Yeah. And Billy rules.

MORE INFO

CATEGORY: Ancient enemy.

APPEARANCE: A flame-shaped ball of fire.

ACCESSORIES: A tall, evil crown that looks like Ice King's.

PERSONALITY: Evil.

POWERS: Fire attacks.

LIKES AND DISLIKES: Likes waging war and kidnapping princesses to marry them or something, we're not exactly sure. Dislikes the ancient hero, Billy.

DO SAY: "You win, Fire Count."

DON'T SAY: "I win!"

FIRE PALACE

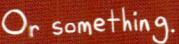

If you were a king made out of fire, where would you want to live? Probably in a castle made out of fire, right? Well, that's exactly where the Flame King lives. It's called the Fire Palace. And it is the hottest place in the whole Fire Kingdom. From there, the Flame King issues his evil fire proclamations. It seems like a lot of the Fire People live in there, too. We don't know how long it's existed. Maybe the Fire Count lived in it. Or maybe Flame King built it. Or something.

It's pretty much your basic castle, except it doesn't have tons of rooms. It might not even have a dungeon or anything. But it definitely has a throne room. In that throne room, there are a couple of giant staircases. The Fire People hang out on those staircases, like to get in good with the Flame King, or do his bidding, or something. We don't know. The Flame King's throne is in there. It is the throne room after all. Above the throne is a little fire lantern, where Flame King used to keep Flame Princess as his prisoner.

The Fire Palace gives me the creeps. It's, like, fifty million degrees in there because everything's on fire or lava. If you're made of fire, it's pretty comfortable, but if you're not made of fire, it's not comfortable at all. It's the opposite of comfortable. It's discomfortable. We're glad Flame Princess escaped from her lantern prison. I wouldn't have wanted to date her if she had to live there still. It'd be too hot. Plus, the Flame King is out of control when he's in his palace. It's like he gets on a power-trip or something.

It makes me want to kick his flame until it's out.

ADVENTUROUS ADVICE
STAYING COOL

If you're ever going to have an adventure in the Fire Kingdom, there's some important stuff you need to know. The Fire Kingdom is so hot that we have to be protected by a heat-proof flame shield to even go there! It's a dangerous place to adventure in, full of evil dudes and flamey weaponry. When you're facing that kind of scary stuff, the most important thing a hero has to know is how to stay cool.

> We should take a loada ice in there next time we go, man!

> That's not quite what I meant by 'staying cool', bro.

Staying cool is an attitude. It's like being brave. Or staying calm. Even when the Flame King launches a mega-fireball attack at you. You just stay calm and say stuff like "Whatever." You know the fireball isn't actually going to hurt you or anything. You gotta have confidence. Everything will be fine. Don't panic.

That's what staying cool is? I can TOTALLY stay cool! I'll stay cool no matter how dangerous our adventures get!

FINN. Seriously. Chill.

I'm a brave adventurer, bro! I can chill AND kick evil butt — don't even worry about it!

Here's something Finn needs to remember about staying cool — it means not losing your temper. Sometimes losing your temper can be a good thing, like if Ice King kidnaps a princess. But when you're just hangin' with your buddies, you shouldn't lose your temper. Just take a couple deep breaths and stay cool. Everyone is happier that way.

Does Flame Princess always lose her temper and stuff because she's made of fire and can't stay cool? Like, literally?

Yup.

REMEMBER THE TIME?

Hey, Jake, remember that time we went to the Fire Kingdom to rescue Cotton Candy Princess from the Fire Count? And we radically used a sword to split him in half!

That wasn't us, Finn. That was Billy.

Shhhh! I know! I just wanted people to think that was us because it was the most righteous amazing mathematical act of all time in the Fire Kingdom!

"No big deal, Finn. We had enough great adventures in the Fire Kingdom that we can remember. Remember that one time when Snow Golem made friends with the Fire Wolf pup, and nearly melted himself into a puddle forever?"

"Oh yeah! And there was that time when Flame Princess made us go back to the Fire Kingdom for her to get her scented candles. What were we thinking?! Scented candles?"

"Yeah, but don't forget that we were able to stop a bunch of bad guys from killing the Flame King. Even though he's evil, he deserves to live – everyone deserves to live. Oh, and we haven't even mentioned the weirdest thing I ever did in the Fire Kingdom . . . The time I went to see Flame Princess and made a fake you, so she'd want to date the real you!"

"Yeah, thanks for that, bro. Things did not work out so good in that relationship. I mean, the first time I ever met Flame Princess, she tried to torch our fort! We did date for a while, but then we broke up and she was really mad at me. You know what it's like to have a girl made out of fire mad at you? They don't forgive or forget. And they try torching all your stuff! And your house! And your best friend!

BONUS ENCOUNTERS

You know, it seems to us like every Kingdom has some people that are kinda tricky to find. The Fire Kingdom is no different. If you happen to see Jalapeno Pepper, Furnius and Torcho, or Flambo, put a tick mark in the box next to them on these pages. And, dude, congratulate yourself on accomplishing something that's real tricky: finding these guys!

JALAPENO PEPPER ☐

A red pepper-looking kinda guy, Jalapeno Pepper is perfect for the Fire Kingdom. He's crazy hot-tempered. And he's a chef, so he uses fire to cook food all the time. You'll know it's him if he's wearing his really tall, white chef's hat. And shouting.

FURNIUS AND TORCHO ☐

Nephews of the Flame King, Furnius and Torcho are balls of fire smaller than their wrongteous uncle. They've been trying to get revenge on Flame King, like, forever for killing their father, who was Flame King's brother. They've even tried to kill the Flame King in the past, but they've always totes failed. They were once disguised as assistants to the Flame King, and wanted to put ice in his ear to extinguish him. Furnius has a creepy forked tongue like a snake and hisses when he speaks, but Torcho speaks without a hiss.

FLAMBO ☐

Flambo is a 'flambit'. That's a hot little flamey creature created when Flame Princess blasts fire at people. Unlike most of the Fire People, Flambo is a good friend. He's always happy to help when we gotta light a fire. And, even

more importantly, he can be a spy in the Fire Kingdom to help us know what Flame King's crazy evil plans are. Most important of all, Flambo can cast a sweet 'flame shield' around us when we go into the Fire Kingdom so we don't get burned by its insane heat.

Burnin' Truth:
A Confessional by Flame Princess

OK, here's the deal. Jake asked me to talk about my relationship with him and Finn. Finn and I have been through times when we haven't wanted to speak to each other ever again! I'll just say that our relationship is . . . **complicated.**

I guess you could say all my relationships are complicated. Like, take my dad, for instance. He's evil and totally overprotective. He kept me prisoner in a freakin' lantern above his throne. For fourteen years! But he's still my dad, you know? I wish he would stop trying to convince me that I'm evil, just because I'm a fire elemental . . .

Then there's Princess Bubblegum. Apparently it was her idea for my dad to put me in that stupid lantern. So now I feel like I can never trust anyone again! Plus she's totally got Finn's heart, so even if I wanted to get back together with him, which I don't, I don't think I could because he's in love with her. That makes things awkward for sure.

And Ice King! Are we enemies? Are we friends? Are we frenemies? You tell me! Wait, actually don't. Finn tricked me into fighting Ice King because of a weird dream he had. But nobody gets to decide stuff like that for me. I'll decide who I fight, who I like and who I don't care about.

Of all the people in Ooo, my relationship with Jake is the least complicated. We're friends, mostly. I know he liked it when I was dating Finn. Him and Flambo helped us meet for the first time! He'd bring us tea and tried to help us stay together, but I guess it wasn't meant to be.

So, that's what I think about Finn and Jake. And actually, I try not to think about them very much. But I kinda end up thinking about them a lot. **It's complicated!**

THE GOOD

CLOUD KINGDOM

RULER: The Cloud People.

INHABITANTS: The Cloud People, The Party God.

GEOGRAPHY: Lots and lots of clouds in the sky.

CLIMATE: Cloudy all the time.

The Cloud Kingdom is unlike any other kingdom in the Land of Ooo, because it doesn't really have a specific ruler. The Cloud People all sort of rule it together somehow. But everybody's really happy there. And why wouldn't they be? They party hard all the time! Actually, the greatest party animal in the Land of Ooo lives there. He's the Party God. We met him once. He looks like a wolf head with a hat on. If you can find him, he'll grant you a wish. That's pretty sweet. Makes going to the Cloud Kingdom worth it. I mean, a wish granted? You don't get that every day. Believe us, we've tried. It's almost impossible.

The Cloud Kingdom is cool, but we wouldn't want to live there all the time. Once, we got kicked out of the Tree Fort and needed to find a place to live. So we looked in the Cloud Kingdom. There was this great-looking house cloud, so we thought we'd check it out. Yeah, dumb choice. There was a cloud person living there with his beautiful cloud bride. They were mean and didn't let us move into their house.

They didn't even offer to help us find a new house! Not cool.

Ah, it's all good, man. We got to go back home to the Tree Fort. What more do you want?

We figured if we lived in the Cloud Kingdom, we'd be partying all the time, and that would actually kinda suck because we wouldn't be able to go on adventures whenever we wanted. Even worse, we might get sick of partying! We don't ever want that to happen to us!

DUCHY OF NUTS

RULER: The Duke and Duchess of Nuts.

INHABITANTS: The Duke and Duchess of Nuts, Marquis of Nuts, Second Nut Son, Peanut People.

GEOGRAPHY: Small portion of the Land of Ooo near the Candy Kingdom (maybe even counts as part of that kingdom) with grass, trees, blue sky, and lots of nuts.

CLIMATE: Warm, sunny.

We don't know if the Duchy of Nuts is exactly part of the Candy Kingdom, but it's sure a lot like the Candy Kingdom, except everything is like nuts, not candy. The houses are nuts, the trees are nuts, the people are nuts. It's ALL NUTS. It's not exactly a kingdom, either, because it's not ruled by a king or princess. It's a duchy or dukedom or whatever, because the Duke and Duchess of Nuts are the rulers there.

We're kinda cool with the Duke of Nuts.

Yeah, but we also feel bad for him, because he has a rare disease – a pudding deficiency. He has to eat a crazy amount of pudding every day, just to stay alive – which sounds awesome, but is apparently pretty difficult. He has to eat sooo many delicious sugary desserts every day that he had to steal some from Princess Bubblegum to have enough to live. She doesn't believe that he even has a disease, so she pretty much hates him for stealing from her.

The Duke is married to the Duchess of Nuts and they have a couple of sons – the Marquis of Nuts and Second Nut Son. The Marquis of Nuts protects and defends his dad. Once, he thought that we were trying to kill the Duke or something, so the Marquis tried to kill us! Not cool. But after one epic fight, he forgave us, and now we're friends, I guess. Second Nut Son is just a baby so doesn't do anything. There's a load of other nut people and peanut people in the duchy, too.

They're pretty good folks, even though they're completely nuts.

HA, HA. NUTS. Get it? They're nuts!

Dude. Stop.

THE GOOD

WILDBERRY KINGDOM

RULER: Wildberry Princess.

INHABITANTS: Wildberry Princess, Wildberry People.

GEOGRAPHY: It's like a giant bush or shrub or tree in the middle of a canyon.

CLIMATE: Perfect harvest weather all year round.

The Wildberry Kingdom is another small kingdom in the Land of Ooo. It's actually a really pretty place if you like bushes and shrubs and stuff. Wildberry Princess is the ruler. She's little and made up of a cluster of berries. If her berries fall off as part of a medical condition, she has to go to the hospital. She lives in the middle of the Wildberry Kingdom. Ice King digs her a lot. We know he digs all the princesses, but he kidnaps her almost as much as Princess Bubblegum.

Almost. But we know he likes kidnapping PB best!

There are also a couple of Wildberry Guards that protect the princess. They look like other types of berries – blueberries, strawberries etc. They are very, very, way too protective of Wildberry Princess. But they don't ever stop Ice King from kidnapping her. We don't get it. I mean, if you're supposed to guard a princess, GUARD THE PRINCESS! Unless they want her to get kidnapped by Ice King.

You know what's also weird about the Wildberry Kingdom? It's all these berry people, and it's in this gardeny, bush and shrub place. But the Wildberry People have a lot of meat. They have meat everywhere! Do they eat it? Are they meat-eating plants? It was handy when Jake had to fake Wildberry Princess's death that one time, but why do they have all that meat everywhere? It really is everywhere! Especially in Wildberry Princess's castle bush house place. That place is basically a giant meat-locker full of steak and chops.

I really, really don't get it!

EVIL FOREST

RULER: N/A.

INHABITANTS: Wall of Flesh, Crystal Guardian, Brain Beast, Skeleton Butterflies.

GEOGRAPHY: It's a forest full of twisted and scary- looking trees.

CLIMATE: A cold chilling air, matching the fear that it radiates.

The Land of Ooo is really big. We still have loooads more places to explore properly. The Evil Forest (or the Evil Dark Forest, as it's sometimes known) is one of those places. We've been there a couple times, but we don't know much about it. What we do know about it is that it's a totally scary place. Even the trees that live there don't wanna be living there! They look like they're being tortured all the time just because it's where they happened to sprout. I feel kinda bad for them.

The forest is the home of the Crystal Apple, too — if you eat it, it takes you to the majorly freaky Crystal Dimension. The Crystal Guardian is a dude who stays there all the time, to make sure no one EVER eats that apple. Seriously, don't even go there. Not even if you're really hungry. The Crystal Dimension is not cool.

The Wall of Flesh lives in the forest, too. He's all gloopy and creepy and is always hiding. He lays around on the ground and then if you step on him, he gets mad and tries to eat you in revenge. When Finn stepped on the Wall of Flesh, he tried to eat Tree Trunks, even though we were both punching him like crazy!

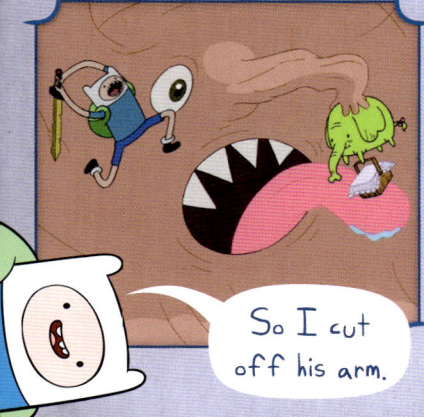

So I cut off his arm.

There's also the skeleton butterflies, which are like butterflies but with skulls for heads. They play music and look a lot eviller than they act. You know who's eviller than they look, though? Sign Zombies. They look like sign posts, because they have signs on the back of their heads. They're vicious and they try to make people leave the Evil Forest, but we fought them and beat them, cause that's what we do!

And don't forget Brain Beast, dude.

Brain Beast is like a pink snake-brain-thing that has a jewel in its face. You break the jewel, you kill the beast. But really you should just avoid the Evil Forest altogether.

LEMONGRAB

RULER: Earl of Lemongrab.

INHABITANTS: Earl of Lemongrab, Lemon Children.

GEOGRAPHY: A small dumb part of the Candy Kingdom. It's very close to the Candy Kingdom, and looks kind of the same, though Lemongrab is mostly on the top of a mountain.

CLIMATE: Bright, cheerful and warm. Unlike the Earl.

So, Lemongrab. What a totally weird place that is. It's kinda part of the Candy Kingdom, but it's sorta independent, too. It's mainly just a lame, grey castle on top of a lame, grey mountain. But what makes Lemongrab creepily unique is that it's ruled by the Earl of Lemongrab.

All that no-good guy wants to do is take over the Candy Kingdom! He's got scarily close a couple times, too, like when Princess Bubblegum got made younger by a magic spell. Lemongrab took over, but when PB was restored to her right age, she kicked his lemony butt out, back to his castle!

That wasn't the end of the Earl, though. Oh noooo. Later, he got lonely and came back to the Candy Kingdom, looking for a pal or a lemon or whatever to spend time with. The problem there is that he basically hates everyone. But he did find a friend eventually — an equally lame clone of himself named Lemongrab 2.

The Earl and Lemongrab 2 lived together and even had weird little Lemon Children, using Princess Bubblegum's scientific formula for creating life. So creepy. Don't even wanna think about it. The Earl is SO EVIL that he forced his Lemon Children to be his slaves and Lemongrab 2 helped free them. That made the Earl angry, so he ate Lemongrab 2. Yup. JUST ATE HIM.

Really, don't think too long or too hard about that one. It's waaaay too messed up.

We hope Lemongrab gets overthrown as soon as possible. In fact, we're waiting for Princess Bubblegum to give the word, and we'll go overthrow him ourselves. But she probably won't tell us to do that anytime soon.

It'd be so sweet, though, if she did . . .

BAD LANDS

RULER: None.

INHABITANTS: Breakfast Kingdom citizens, Slime Kingdom citizens, hobos.

GEOGRAPHY: On the outskirts of the Land of Ooo.

CLIMATE: Cloudy but sunny above the clouds.

When you live in a place like the Land of Ooo where there are a lot of different kingdoms, you need somwhere where the rulers can all get together for important ceremonies, and to talk about stuff. In Ooo, that place is the Royal Congressional Hall in the Bad Lands. It's way up in the clouds and looks like a weird sorta tree house. Apart from this hall, there's not much else worth looking at in the Bad Lands. The Slime Kingdom and the Breakfast Kingdom are round these parts, but they're both pretty small. All in all, the Bad Lands are kinda empty.

Except for the hobos and bandits who wander around. Don't forget about those guys.

Some of the ceremonies and stuff that go on in the Royal Congressional Hall are things like the Back Rubbing Ceremony. All the rulers give each other back rubs. This is weirdly like the most important ceremony in the Land of Ooo. PB won't let us take part. Mean.

They even eat Princess Bubblegum's special royal tarts there and NOWHERE ELSE. One time, PB assigned us to make sure the tarts made it to the ceremony. They're delivered by following the Royal Tart Path, which leads from the Bad Lands to the Candy Kingdom. It's like the easiest path to walk down ever.

They also have the Grand Meeting of Ooo Royalty there. We don't know what they talk about, because we've never been, but actually we don't care. It sounds lame. It's probably a lot of dumb politics stuff. Booooorrrrriiiiinnnggggg! If it's not having an adventure or leading to an adventure, I'm not interested.

THE UGLY

BENEATHAVERSE

RULER: Gnome Ruler.

INHABITANTS: Grandmaster of the Gnomes, Gnome henchmen.

GEOGRAPHY: Underground, dark, rocky, no light, generally AWFUL.

CLIMATE: Kinda sheltered from climate. Because it's underground. Duh.

Ugh. This place. Seriously. We've only been to the Beneathaverse one time, but believe us, that was plenty time enough. The Beneathaverse is a tiny, underground town where the Gnome Ruler and his creepy little Gnome citizens live. In the dark, in weird little wooden houses. You can get there by climbing down the well next to the Tree Fort.

Or you can get there by being dragged down the well against your will. While being prodded with a giant taser.

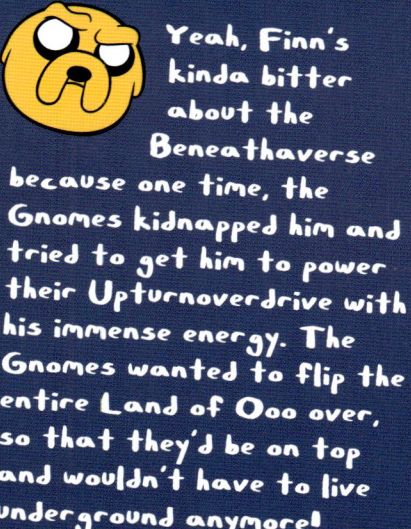

Yeah, Finn's kinda bitter about the Beneathaverse because one time, the Gnomes kidnapped him and tried to get him to power their Upturnoverdrive with his immense energy. The Gnomes wanted to flip the entire Land of Ooo over, so that they'd be on top and wouldn't have to live underground anymore!

They made me run in a giant hamster wheel, dude. It was definitely not cool.

I can kinda see why the Gnomes hated it down there, though. There was no sunshine, or grass, or sky, or animals, or fun . . . I'd wanna flip that lair over, too, if I had to live in that cave!

Yeah, well, I accidentally destroyed the entire lair by dancing around too much anyway. So who even cares.

THE UGLY

DESERT OF DOOM

RULER: None.

INHABITANTS: Taddle, Grimby, Chuds.

GEOGRAPHY: Sandy, desert, near the Bad Lands, separated by a mountain range.

CLIMATE: Hot, dry. Desert-y.

You know what we think is the least algebraic, ugliest place in the Land of Ooo? It's the Desert of Doom. It's all sandy and hot and miserable. There's all these ugly dead animal carcasses, but nobody even knows what kinda weird animals they were before they died. They probably got exploded during the Mushroom War or something. But they make the Desert of Doom extra ugly. We've been there a couple times. The absolute worst was when we had to deliver the tarts to the Royal Back Rubbing Ceremony.

We were dumb to carry the tarts through that LAME desert.

Seriously, the Desert of Doom is a dangerous place filled with hobos, thieves, murderers (probably), and just a whole bunch of bad guys. When we were taking the tarts to the ceremony, we fought some of the hobos and thieves like Grimby, Tattle, and JJ.

We smoothly outsmarted them, though. They thought they got away with the Royal Tarts, but we gave them poisoned ones. They were never heard from again. OOPS.

We also met the Chuds. They're these butt-ugly monsters that live in a cave and want to steal tarts, too. We fought them off, but they got a couple tarts away from us. They have gotta be the ugliest part of the Desert of Doom.

Yeah bro, seriously, their eyes have fallen out, and they just want to kill you for your tarts.

Stupid desert. Stupid Chuds and thieves and hobos. There's even a butterfly that has a laser gun in this crazy-creepy desert. What? He stole some tarts, too. He's just like everyone else who lives in the Desert of Doom. Nasty, evil and especially ugly. We shoulda known the desert was going to be so ugly, because it's really close to the Bad Lands, and there's not much there that's any good either. Stupid desert.

THE UGLY

LICH'S LAIR

RULER: The Lich.

INHABITANTS: The Lich.

LANDSCAPE/GEOGRAPHY: Underground tunnels.

CLIMATE: Dark, underground.

Do you know the Lich? That guy is the worst! He's super creepy-looking. He's got a skeleton face, big horns and can do evil magic. He only wants to destroy EVERY LIVING THING in the Land of Ooo. No big deal. We make sure we stop him every time he tries something completely evil. He's at his most annoying when he controls people's minds and makes them attack you. He possessed Princess Bubblegum one time, but we freed her and beat him, as usual. Because we rule. YEAH.

Ugh! The Lich! This dude is 100% our mortal enemy!

What's worse than him is the disgusting place he lives in. He calls it the Lich's Lair, but it's not really a lair or a castle or anything. It's a dump. It's these underground tunnels and stuff that were probably built before the Mushroom War.

They're gross. Also they smell like...

Let's just say they smell sick.

In his Lair, the no-good Lich has a Well of Power. It's a big well (duh, obviously) filled with toxic juicy stuff that drips down from a pipe high above in the ceiling. The Well gives the Lich his wrongetous evil powers, which is the whole reason why he bothers to live in gross underground tunnels. He has to protect his Well, so he has a whole load of Skeleton Guards to help him out. We're pretty sure they come from the Desert of Doom. Anyway, they're these creepy dead skeleton guys who fight to keep the Well and the Lair safe from good, heroic adventurers like us.

It's no fun to fight the Lich, because he can't die. All our worst enemies can't die, like the Lich and Death. But it's all good. We still kick their butts and stop their evil plans. That's what adventurers and warriors do. Beat the bad guys! Yeeeeaaaah!

FIGHTING

When we go on adventures, we know that we're probably gonna have to fight some evil. We have to fight bad guys all the time. And fights can be really brutal. You have to make sure you're in the right before you fight. If you're fighting and you're wrong, that's the worst thing in the world. Really you should just fight to protect yourself and other people you love from being attacked by evil, wrongteous dudes. And monsters. Always fight monsters.

I love adventuring. It's my favourite thing. And I'm always right, so it's always OK for me to fight bad guys. I don't fight when I'm wrong. But also, I'm never wrong.

So it's all good.

If you're going to fight on adventures, you have to be prepared. You get prepared by exercising and eating a healthy diet. Especially if you're going to fight monsters. Monsters don't eat a healthy diet. They eat people and souls and stuff — that has zero nutritional value. And exercise will help you be ready and in shape for the fight. You don't want to get so tired halfway through the fight that you have to quit, have a nap and lose the fight!

That would be embarrassing!

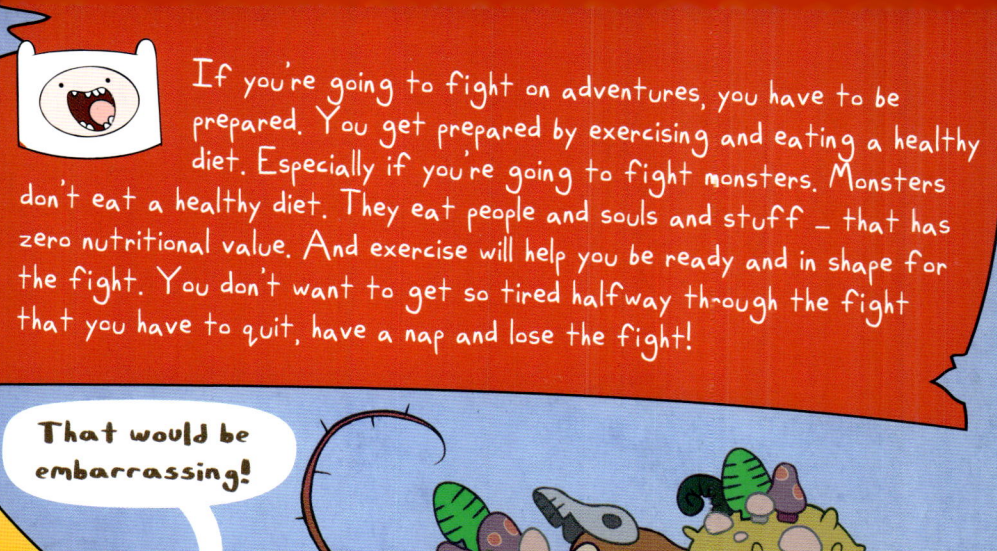

Also, you have to have some smarts if you want to fight. You need to use your brain to think about the kinds of attacks you're going to do, and to figure out where the monster is vulnerable. If you don't know how to use your brain to figure out this stuff, you'll probably lose the fight, too. And monsters are dumb! Don't let them outthink you! You're smart. You'll figure it out. And then you'll win.

ADVENTURE TIME!

That's why you need to prepare first. So you can win at the right time.

In preparation for fighting a whole load of evil on our adventures, I like to carry a sword. They're my favourite weapon and I have a bunch that I like to use.

GOLDEN SWORD:

This was my favourite for a long time. I used it in battle so much that it got all banged up and broken. Actually, it got exploded.

ROOT SWORD:

This one is good, but the handle is kind of annoying. It's made out of a couple of roots that have grown together.

DEMON SWORD:

This was my main sword for a while. It was from Jake's dad's dungeon and it was crazy powerful. It was made of demon blood, which isn't as gross as it sounds. The demon blood made it awesome! It was immune to Marceline's blood mist cloud and even fire.

 I use other swords now, like the grass sword, which replaced my demon sword after I broke it . . . and then there's the steel sword, the Sword of the Dead, the dual swords, and katanas! Jake has a sword he uses sometimes, too, but he mostly likes to use his powers to fight stuff, and not weapons so much.

 Sometimes when I fight I use other kinds of weapons too, not just swords. I like daggers, sai, and even used a shark, although that was kind of a sword. I'm cool with using a crossbow sometimes, too.

Even though there are a lot of weapons to use when you fight, you have to remember that it's not the weapons that make the difference — it's the person using them! It's all about you, baby! If you're in shape, have a lot of energy and are smart, you'll win the fight even if you don't have the best weapons.

Yeah, that!

THE ENCHIRIDION

When you go adventuring, it's a good idea to do your research and listen to wise heroic advice. That's why one of the best adventuring accessories we ever had was the Enchiridion — an ancient book that tells you all the stuff you need to know to become a kick-butt hero.

Intense-looking bird.

Old, dusty cover, kinda sticky (Finn's fault).

Too many bookmarks.

Awesome skull and sword arrangement.

Shields of some description.

Grapes. No idea what they have to do with anything.

Mysterious numbers 8, 13 and 21 on the back.

This book was sweet. Princess Bubblegum sent us on a quest to find it and we had to face a whole load of heroic trials along the way. We crossed lava pits and fought an ogre on our path to the Enchiridion, but it was totally worth it. Although, we kinda didn't realize how powerful it was for a while.

We might have used the Enchiridion for sitting on when the grass was wet . . . but as soon as we found out it could open wormholes between dimensions and stuff, we were totally into it. It had chapters on loads of cool, essential hero stuff. Like how Cyclops tears can heal any wound, and how to avoid pitfalls and traps.

And how to kiss princesses. Finn.

Shut up, dude. I don't even know what kissing you're talking about.

If nothing else, the Enchiridion was pretty heavy, so you could always use it to hit your evil enemies. Sadly, Finn had to smash it up when that wrongteous heap o' evil the Lich got hold of it.

That was no fun. But sometimes a hero's gotta do what a hero's gotta do.

CHARACTER CHECKLIST

You gotta be so good at spotting stuff if you wanna see EVERYONE who wanders around the Land of Ooo. I mean, there are rare folk, and then there are like crazy-rare folk who it's almost impossible to get a look at!

See if you can spot any of the guys and gals and weird creature-type-things on this list. If you do see them, put a tick mark in the box next to their picture. And congratulate yourself on being the most mathematical of heroic adventurers.

A

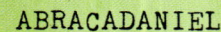

□ ABRACADANIEL

□ ABRAHAM LINCOLN

□ AMOEBA

□ AQUANDRIUS

□ ASH:

Ugh we HATE this dude. He's Marceline's loser ex-boyfriend. One -ime, he sold her teddy bear, Hambo! Evil. We're glad they broke up.

x

168

B

☐ BADLEMONNOHOPE

☐ BALLOON CREATURES

☐ BELLAMY BOY

☐ BETTY

☐ BIG DESTINY

☐ BLANKET DRAGON

☐ BLASTRONAUT

☐ BOB RAINICORN

☐ BOOBAFINA

☐ BOOBOO

☐ BREAKFAST PEOPLE:

These delicious-looking citizens of Ooo are made of breakfast-y treats. Ice King is always bothering their royal sisters, Toast Princess and Breakfast Princess.

☐ BUFO

☐ BUSINESSMEN

☐ CHOOSE GOOSE:

Goose and merchant of weird, mostly useless stuff. Although he did give me some cool glasses once that made me super-smart. Talks in rhyme almost always.

C

☐ CACTUS CREATURES

☐ CHERRY CREAM SODA

CLOWN
NURSES

COLONEL
CANDY CORN

COSMIC
OWL

CRYSTAL
GUARDIAN

CUBER

CUTE KING

D

DOCTOR
PRINCESS:

Doctor
of the
Land of
Ooo, who
was captured
by Ice King, but
then turned out
not to be an
actual princess.
Princess is just
her last name!
Her alter-ego is
Science Whyzard.

DIMENSION
WIZARD

DOOR LORD

E

EBERHARDT

ELDER PLOPS

DR J

F

FEAR
FEASTER

FIGHT KING

FLAME
MINSTREL

🟧 FOREST
CYCLOPS

🟧 FOREST
WIZARD

🟧 FRUIT
WITCH

⬜ GARY THE
MERMAID
QUEEN

⬜ GEORGY

⬜ GOLIAD:

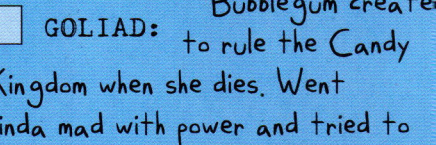

A pink
sphinx-
type
thing
that Princess
Bubblegum created
to rule the Candy
Kingdom when she dies. Went
kinda mad with power and tried to
psychically control everyone.

⬜ GRAND
MASTER
WIZARD

⬜ GROB GOB
GLOB GROD

⬜ GUARDIAN
ANGEL

⬜ GUMMY

H

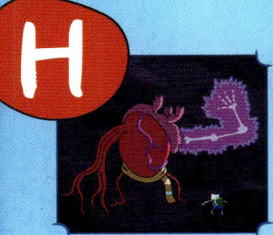

🟥 THE HEART
BEAST

🟥 HAMBURGER
MONSTER

🟥 HUG WOLVES

I

🟪 THE IRON
OWL

J

🟩 JAYBIRD

🟩 JELLY BEAN
PEOPLE

🟩 JERMAINE

🟩 JIGGLER

JOSHUA & MARGARET:
My mom and dad! They adopted Finn when he was a tiny baby, making us the best of bros forever and ever. I love these guys.

KEE-OTH

KEY-PER

LASER WIZARD

LITTLE DUDE

MAGIC MAN

MANFRIED THE TALKING PINATA

MILDWIN

MINI QUEEN

THE MORROW: PB's gigantic pet falcon that she flies around on sometimes, to get to ceremonies and whatever else it is that she does. Princessy stuff.

MOUNTAIN MAN

NAKED WIZARD

NEVER-ENDING PIE-THROWING ROBOT

OLD SWANS

P

☐ PAPER PETE

☐ PARTY PAT

☐ PHIL THE PYJAMA NINJA

☐ PIG

Q

☐ QUILTON

R

☐ RICARDIO:

Ugh. This guy. He's the Ice King's heart, brought to life. For a while we thought he might marry Princess Bubblegum, but then he tried to cut out her heart. Not cool.

☐ ROCK WIZARD

☐ RON JAMES

☐ ROOT BEER GUY

☐ ROYAL TART PATH GUARD

☐ ROYAL TART TOTER

☐ RUMP PEOPLE

S

☐ SCIENCE

☐ SCORCHER

☐ SHARON

☐ SHOKO

☐ SIR SLICER

☐ SNORLOCK

As strong as her name suggests, Susan can crush boulders with her bare hands. We thought she was a human, but it turned out she was a Hyooman. Totally different thing.

SUSAN STRONG:

SUPER FREAK

T

TIFFANY

TREE WITCH

TWO-HEADED CUTIE

U

UGLY MONSTER

ULTIMATE WIZARD

V

VEGGIE PEOPLE

W

WENDY

WHISPER DAN

WIZARD THIEF

WORM KING

X

Mean, weird little goblin king who treated his citizens real bad. But we defeated him in the end. OBVIOUSLY.

XERGIOK:

Z

ZAP

So, there you have it. You now know pretty much everything there is to know about the Land of Ooo. You know about all the kingdoms. You know about all our friends. You know about all our enemies. But we're still exploring Ooo and going on new adventures all the time, so who knows what other cool stuff we'll know about in the future?

Don't forget all the advice you got from reading this book. You know all about romance, adventuring, Promcoming, friendship, food, even being evil. If you need reminders about all this stuff, you can pick up this book again, and read it again, and again, and again, and again. AND AGAIN. It's a pretty important book to read.

You're totally ready to come to the Land of Ooo and go on adventures with me and Jake. That is, if you're righteous enough. We're waiting for you. We'll see you next time!

And what time is that?

ADVENTURE TIME!